MOTIVATIONAL INTERVIEWING FOR LEADERSHIP: MI-LEAD

BY

JASON WILCOX, LCSW

BRIAN C. KERSH, PHD

ELIZABETH JENKINS, PHD

Gray Beach Publishing

Motivational Interviewing for Leadership: MI-LEAD

Copyright ©2017 by Gray Beach Publishing

All rights reserved as permitted under the U.S. Copyright Act of 1976, no part of this publication may be reproduced, distributed, or transmitted in any form or by any means, or stored in a database or retrieval system, without the prior permission of the publisher.

Gray Beach Publishing
2017

First Edition: 2017

The characters, names, incidents, organizations, dialogue, and events portrayed in this book are fictitious when identified as such. Any similarity to a real person, living or dead is coincidental and not intended by the authors. Names have been changed to protect the privacy of others in the true stories.

Motivational Interviewing for Leadership: MI-LEAD
by Jason Wilcox, LCSW, Brian C. Kersh, PhD, Elizabeth Jenkins, PhD

ISBN-13: **978-1542447683** (pbk)

Cover design by Jason Wilcox

Edited by Brian Kersh, PhD, Elizabeth Jenkins, PhD, & Michelle Drapkin, PhD

Printed in the United States of America

This book is dedicated to

Dr. Michael Goldstein

&

Dr. Margaret Dundon

Who are inspiring mentors and exemplars of transformational leadership

Table of Contents

Section I Overview and Background

1 Transformational Leadership and Motivational Interviewing — 2

2 Background of MI and Overview — 13

3 Why MI-LEAD — 27

Section II Skill Development and Exercises

4 Spirit of MI — 34

5 Four Processes in MI — 44

6 MI Core Skills (OARS) — 51

7 Working through Ambivalence — 72

8 Dancing with Discord — 89

9 Planning: How does it fit? — 120

Section III Other

10 Ethical Considerations — 132

11 Summary and Wrap-up — 145

Epilogue: Where the Goose Leads — 152

Reference Page — 166

CHAPTER 1

Transformational Leadership and Motivational Interviewing

When you think of a successful leader, what characteristics come to mind? Do you think of someone who rules with an iron fist, an individual who dictates what followers must do, who displays little tolerance for disagreement, and who uses punishment as a motivator? Or do you instead envision an individual who inspires followers to be their best, who fosters individual growth and excellence, and who works closely with followers to determine the best path forward for the team? If your vision of a successful leader more closely matches the latter, then you're already in tune with *Transformational Leadership* and *Motivational Interviewing*.

Transformational Leadership

So, what is transformational leadership? The theory of Transformational Leadership was introduced in the late 1970s (Burns, 1978) and expanded upon across the following two decades (Bass & Avolio, 1995). It is a leadership style that emphasizes collaboration with those being led and a focus on their well-being as a path to enhancing organizational success. A transformational leader believes that a well-engaged, intrinsically-driven group of individuals is key to an organization's ability to thrive. Thus, the transformational leader is someone who demonstrates concern and compassion for his followers and motivates and challenges them to be their best. A particularly important component of transformational leadership is termed "individualized consideration," in which an effective leader *engages* those he leads and *seeks to understand* and value their needs, strengths, and goals. Through transformational leadership, a leader empowers others and increases their self-efficacy while emphasizing a *shared mission*, which enhances creativity and motivation and results in improved organizational performance.

So, what's the point? Does it really matter what style a leader exhibits, as long as the trains run on time? Well, it turns out leadership style has quite an impact—in terms of organizational success, follower performance, and leader satisfaction.

In the business setting, research has demonstrated a strong relation between transformational leadership and employee and organizational performance, individual creativity, and organizational innovation (Dvir, 2002; Howell & Avolio 1993, Low 1996; Gumusluoglu & Ilsev; Bass 1995; Jung 2001). Fortune and the Great Place to Work Institute annually publish Fortune's *100 Best Companies to Work For®*, based on a survey of employees at over 250 companies. According to this survey, factors that consistently contribute to a "best" company include having a company culture of trust, a clearly defined company mission, positive working relationships with colleagues and management, opportunities for advancement within the company, and a work environment that fosters a sense of pride and responsibility, all of which are elements that transformational leadership promotes. Intrinsic motivation and self-efficacy are believed to relate to employee creativity and are influenced by factors such as employee perception of support for innovation (Scott & Bruce, 1994), a feeling of empowerment (Deci, 1989), and the employee perception of the work environment (Amabile, 1983, 1996, 1998; Tierney 1999). All of these factors are influenced by employee relationships with their leaders.

As demonstrated by the above findings, when business leaders create an atmosphere of trust, positive working relationships among staff at all levels, responsibility, and empowerment, employees are more engaged, creative, and satisfied. The benefits of such a workforce are many and include superior financial performance, enhanced innovation, lowered compliance risk, and reduced employee turnover. A motivated workforce is essential to an organization's long-term success, and leaders are an integral part of assuring that employees are engaged and satisfied, that they are knowledgeable about the company's mission, that they trust their leadership, and that they experience a sense of ownership for the products or services provided. Transformational leaders develop this important relationship between leader and employee, resulting in enhanced employee satisfaction and employee sense of ownership for outcomes, both of which increase organizational success.

So what's in it for the transformational leader, other than a successful organization and an engaged, creative, productive, and satisfied group of followers? As you may not be surprised to hear, given the above, transformational leaders are more satisfied than their more autocratic leaders. In addition, employer satisfaction negatively predicts professional employee turnover (Jawahar & Hemmase, 2006). It is easy to see why, when your organization is successful and your followers are engaged and satisfied, you as a leader benefit too. This is not only true in the business world, but in other settings too. For instance, clinicians who practice medicine using an approach that is consistent with transformational leadership, an approach we'll discuss in more detail throughout this book, experience improved team cohesion and less burnout (Pollak et al., 2015). Moreover, when nursing supervisors adopt this same approach, their employees describe themselves as more satisfied with their jobs (Medley & Larochelle, 1995). Similarly, employees working under a transformational leader achieve greater job success (Riaz & Haider, 2010) and stay at their jobs longer (Dunham, 1990).

While many of the examples and research indicated above come from the business world, it should be noted that transformational leadership is a model for leaders in any setting, whether it is the workplace, politics, sports, religious organizations, or any other setting where leaders lead. Before we leave the business world entirely and focus on leaders more generally, it may be worth considering some well-known models of management and their relation to transformational leadership.

Management Styles

Many different management models have been described and studied over the years, and we review several of these below. These various models differ, sometimes widely, in their perspectives on the role of management in employee motivation and around worker perceptions of their role in an organization. Some of these models closely match the transformational leadership perspective; their premise is that satisfied, autonomous employees are productive employees and that leaders need to facilitate a company culture of trust, communicate a clearly defined company mission, foster positive working relationships with colleagues and management, and provide both opportunities for advancement within the company and a work environment that fosters a sense of pride and responsibility. Others have opposing views of both leaders and their followers.

Douglas McGregor presented Theory X and Theory Y in 1960. These two well-known theories make very different assumptions about what underlies worker motivation. Theory X assumes that workers are inherently unmotivated ("lazy") and will generally attempt to avoid engaging in work if possible. Theory Y, in contrast, assumes that workers are inherently creative and derive pleasure from work. Theory X has been termed an "Autocratic Style", and Theory Y has been termed a "Participative Style" (DuBrin, 1990). Others describe these styles as "hard" versus "soft" management, respectively (Benson, 2015).

According to Theory X, since workers will attempt to avoid work when possible, some type of pressure or coercion is necessary if workers are going to be productive. A rigid management style, threats of disciplinary action and monetary incentives are viewed as necessary for maintaining employee motivation and productivity.

Very little attention is paid to the employee's creativity, ideas, or goals, and managers sacrifice employee satisfaction, engagement, and creativity within a Theory X style of management.

In contrast, Theory Y managers view the relationship between the workers and management as important. This is a more popular management theory, and it assumes that workers enjoy work that allows for creativity, independence, and responsibility. This type of management style involves the workers in the decision-making process and organizational planning. A Theory Y manager shares decision-making with the group either by allowing workers to vote on decisions or by facilitating group discussions that lead to a decision that reflects the group consensus (DuBrin, 2010).

A third management style has been offered by William Ouchi (1981). Theory Z is specifically focused on workers' perceptions of management and management's perceptions of workers. This management style, which reflects aspects of the Japanese culture, views workers as participating more actively and as able to perform a large range of different tasks. These workers are believed to desire close and collaborative working relationships with their managers. They are viewed as disciplined, hard workers who can be trusted to give their best in the workplace and who expect organizational support for family and traditions. The goal with this type of leadership style is to engender employee loyalty and knowledge about the organization as a whole. Workers are expected to remain with the organization and ultimately help train new employees using the same managerial model (Luthans, 2007). Both Theory Y and Theory Z view managers as coaches who encourage worker participation and productivity. These two managerial styles support a workplace environment that fosters engaged and motivated employees who are knowledgeable about the company's mission, have trust in their leadership, and experience a sense of ownership for the products or services provided.

Leadership has also been conceptualized and categorized along several archetypes or styles, including *transformational*, *empowering*, *directive*, *transactional*, and *aversive*. Transformational leadership and empowering leadership styles have been associated with increased job satisfaction (Bass, 1985; Hater & Bass, 1988; Howell & Frost, 1989; Koh, Steers, & Terborg, 1995; Ross & Offermann, 1997; Sosik, 1997; Yun, Cox, & Sims, 2007). Both are democratic types of leadership that consider the needs of the individual employees in contrast with other archetypes that tend to be more autocratic and focused specifically on the organizational or leader's agenda rather than the employees goals. Autocratic styles such as directive and transactional leadership styles have not been related to job satisfaction, while an aversive leadership style is negatively associated with job satisfaction (Yun, Cox, & Sims, 2007).

As transformational leadership continues to be examined in terms of employee productivity, satisfaction, and organizational success, a related leadership style has been identified, *Empowering Leadership* or *Self-Leadership*, which shifts the paradigm towards a management style that emphasizes employee self-influence rather than a top-down influence (Manz & Sims, 1990; 1991). This style of management values the unique input of individual employees, each of whom is his own self-manager (Ahearne, Matthieu, & Rapp; 2005; Pearce & Sims, 2002; Pearce, Yoo, & Alavi, 2004; Yun, Cox, & Sims, 2006; Yun, Faraj, & Sims, 2005), and while distinct from the transformational leadership model, Self-Leadership continues to emphasize the importance of each individual employee's input to support organizational success.

Another management model that, like Theory Z, has emerged from the Japanese business culture is *Lean Management*, derived from *Lean Manufacturing* processes, initially developed by the Toyota automotive company (Teich & Faddoul, 2013). Lean manufacturing processes promote a culture of continuous improvement and do so in large part by focusing on eliminating waste in the manufacturing process. So what does this have to do with Transformational Leadership? Lean managers rely upon their employees to identify wasteful practices, and they empower their employees to participate in the improvement process. They recognize that continuous improvement and, ultimately, the success of the company are only possible to the extent that the workforce is active, engaged, and empowered when it comes to identifying and eliminating waste and improving the overall flow of manufacturing processes. As such, lean managers function more as coaches than as autocrats.

Another leadership style worth highlighting here is *servant leadership*. While the above models are more closely tied to management and the business world, servant leadership is a more broadly defined leadership model and perhaps most closely embodies transformational leadership as we see it. According to Robert Greenleaf, who coined the term "servant leadership" in a 1970 essay, "The difference [between servant-first and leader-first] manifests itself in the care taken by the servant-first to make sure that other people's highest priority needs are being served. The best test, and difficult to administer, is: Do those served grow as persons? Do they, while being served, become healthier, wiser, freer, more autonomous, more likely themselves to become servants?" As you can see in this quote, servant leaders are primarily driven by the needs of those they serve; the emphasis is on the growth and development of those served rather than promoting the needs of the leader.

Transformational Leadership and Management Style

Remembering the annual employee satisfaction survey discussed above, we see that worker engagement and a culture of both trust and mutual support are integral in reducing employee turnover, increasing creativity, ensuring superior financial performance and productivity, and reducing risk. Effective leaders communicate a clearly defined company mission as well as seek to understand and respect the values, needs, and goals of the employees. The result is an engaged and intrinsically motivated workforce.

Aspects of motivation in the workplace including employee engagement, creativity, productivity, and job satisfaction are not driven solely by the employee but also by the work environment AND the relationship between the employee and his supervisors. Leadership style is a fundamental aspect of employee motivation, which is, perhaps, good news and bad news. The good news is that there are things that can be done to increase employee motivation! However, we as leaders are an integral part of these efforts and thus carry a degree of responsibility when there is low employee engagement, creativity, productivity, and/or job satisfaction. The bottom line is that we as leaders *can* and *do* have a significant impact on employee motivation.

So, from the business world and beyond, we see models of management that are both consistent (i.e., Theory Y, Theory Z, lean management, servant leadership) and inconsistent (Theory X, autocratic leadership) with transformational leadership, and we see the benefits to organizations, employees, and leaders when a more transformational leadership style is used. But, as we noted previously, leaders are not solely within the business world. Leaders are found within a wide variety of settings, and the same characteristics that make a leader effective in the business world can make a leader effective in these other settings as well.

Motivational Interviewing

Motivational Interviewing for Leadership (MI-Lead) is an adaptation of Motivational Interviewing (MI) that focuses on specific approaches that leaders can embody to become transformational leaders. MI is defined as "a collaborative, goal-oriented style of communication with particular attention to the language of change. It is designed to strengthen personal motivation for and commitment to a specific goal by eliciting and exploring the person's own reasons for change within an atmosphere of acceptance and compassion" (Miller & Rollnick, 2012). Much like individualized consideration in transformational leadership, MI emphasizes *engaging* and *listening* with an ear for understanding and valuing the individual's needs, strengths, and goals. It is an approach that focuses on collaborating with others, drawing upon their strengths, and placing their best interests on par with, if not ahead of, one's own. It also recognizes that the ultimate choice around change is up to the individual, not the leader, and explicitly honors the individual's choice to change or stay the same.

MI was originally introduced in the 1980's after William Miller was asked by colleagues to describe his very successful, client-centered approach in working with individuals engaging in substance abuse. Since then, MI has been widely studied as a means of facilitating motivation for many types of behavior change by eliciting an individual's own reasons for change and by addressing importance, confidence, and readiness for change. This approach has not only demonstrated effectiveness at helping individuals quit abusing substances, it has also proven to be effective in the areas of health-related behavior change (such as increased physical activity, improved diet, and medication adherence (Hettema, Steele, & Miller, 2005)), public health (such as HIV risk reduction and community adoption of safe water storage practices (Hettema, Steele, & Miller, 2005)), and the legal system (such as reducing parole violations (Anstiss, 2011)). The more widely MI has been implemented and studied, the more we are seeing how effective it is at promoting positive change in multiple behavioral domains across various settings.

Motivational Interviewing and Transformational Leadership

So, what does MI have to do with transformational leadership? As a leader, you may have found yourself in a situation in which you have an exciting new idea, and in your enthusiasm to share your exciting new idea and ways to implement it, you lose the interest of those you are attempting to inspire. Perhaps you have found that the more you attempt to convince others about the merits of a plan, the more they respond with talk about barriers, or the more they point out the limitations of your idea. What has happened in these situations that has caused your wonderfully well-thought out plan to end with the disengagement of those you're leading or outright rejection of your idea?

While you as a leader bring a vision for the changes needed in an organization, those you lead are essential in that they must feel a sense of ownership in the vision and process for the changes, coming up with, or at minimum collaborating to come up with, the solutions and goals for change in order for the plan to succeed. If others are going to be fully engaged in implementing the plan, they will need to find their own reasons to value the plan and identify solutions that can bring about the change or vision. While you and those you lead are seeking a shared mission, or the "WHAT" in your goals, your role as their leader is to assist them in finding their own "WHY" for following through with behaviors that support those goals. By understanding their agendas or reasons for engaging in a particular behavior, their "WHY," you can work collaboratively to develop a "HOW" or plan for following through with the identified goals.

MI's emphasis on eliciting the reasons for change from an individual rather than implanting one's own reasons for change into that individual is not a new one, and, as noted above, research is increasingly demonstrating the broad reach of this effective style of interacting with an individual and increasing his or her likelihood of engaging in a particular behavior. In short, MI is effective at engaging others in the process of making positive change. With MI-Lead, leaders have begun to adopt the MI approach within healthcare and other organizational settings as a means of enhancing individual motivation for and engagement in behaviors that lead to individual, group, department, and/or organizational success.

MI-Lead is a model for transformational leadership designed to facilitate engagement and motivation for behavior and system change. It is a style of leadership that emphasizes asking and listening with a focus on organizational goals, the leader's goals, AND the goals of those being led. The relationship between leader and those being led involves trust, empowerment, and confidence building. The outcomes include increased engagement, productivity, and willingness to assume responsibility for tasks/projects, as well as reduced attrition.

Finally, it should be noted that the MI leadership approach can be learned. While some may be born transformational leaders, others can become such leaders by learning and implementing the MI approach. Considerable research has been conducted in the area of learning MI, and we have used this research to inform our training of leaders and our approach in this book, which provides a strong foundation in the MI-Lead style. Those who are not born transformational leaders will notice that in addition to learning and implementing the material in this book, considerable time spent practicing and getting feedback around this approach will be necessary to being able to implement it proficiently. We will discuss strategies for getting additional practice and feedback in this approach later in this book, for those who are interested.

In summary, an engaged and motivated team is essential to an organization's success. Leadership plays an important role in individual satisfaction and willingness to engage in behavior change with a sense of pride and responsibility for the success of the organization. An eliciting leadership style, one that supports individual creativity and autonomy while communicating a shared mission, is particularly effective. Transformational leaders are ones who demonstrate an interest in and concern for the values, needs, and beliefs of the individuals they lead and are more likely to evoke from those individuals behaviors that support the growth of the organization by increasing engagement and motivation. MI-Lead incorporates the fundamental principles of MI into a leadership approach that provides the tools to engage and motivate others, facilitating their knowledge about the organization's mission, encouraging trust in their leadership, and increasing their sense of ownership for their organization's impact. The following chapters will provide an overview of motivational interviewing and ways to effectively incorporate aspects of MI-Lead into your organization.

CHAPTER 2

Background of MI and Overview

As we indicated in the initial chapter, our framework for helping to develop transformational leaders is Motivational Interviewing (MI), a communication style that fosters change. In this chapter, we describe the foundational attitude (*way of being* in the presence of others), the roadmap for implementation, and the essential skills associated with MI. We also review some concepts that are important for understanding and applying MI. This chapter will provide a brief, general outline of the MI approach. Later, we'll describe how MI aligns with transformational leadership and discuss specific strategies for putting MI-Lead into practice.

Miller and Rollnick (2012), the developers of MI, describe it as a "collaborative conversation for strengthening a person's own motivation and commitment to change" (page 12). MI was originally developed in the 1980s as a clinical approach to treat substance use disorders. It was so effective in this area, especially relative to standard approaches at that time, that it quickly spread to other areas involving health-related behavior change (for example, tobacco cessation, medication adherence, diet, exercise, and HIV risk reduction). MI has now expanded beyond health care and is being used by other organizations and systems that are interested in promoting behavior change that supports the well-being of others, for example, in the legal system and in corporate leadership.

What makes MI so different from the traditional (or standard) approach to promoting change in the substance use disorder, primary care, legal, and leadership settings? In each of these settings, the common practice for many years has been to encourage behavior change (for example, eliminating substance use, eating healthier, or obeying the restrictions of parole) by having an authority figure persuade, advise, and/or threaten the individual for whom change would be beneficial, often by the authority figure extolling the many benefits of change and/or warning of the dire consequences of not changing. This style may sound familiar, since this model of affecting change is analogous to the Theory X managerial style discussed in the previous chapter. The fundamental difference between MI and these traditional approaches is the focus on enhancing the individual's *own* motivation for change. That is, instead of an external factor forcing motivation in an individual who otherwise lacks it, the MI approach is to seek, elicit, and enhance the motivation already within an individual. This monumental difference in attitude and approach has been so effective in promoting change in the settings noted above that it has become the gold standard within many organizations (for example, many large, primary and secondary health care systems). This is an important, critical difference in approach and is fundamental to the success of MI. Let's explore further.

MI Spirit

Miller and Rollnick refer to the underlying attitude of MI noted above as the "spirit" of MI. They describe the four necessary components of the MI spirit as partnership, acceptance, compassion, and evocation. *Partnership* involves the active promotion of teamwork and collaboration. It is the *explicit* recognition that each member of the team brings valuable elements to the table and that each deserves a say in the plan for behavior change. This does not mean that all team members have the same level of expertise and/or power, but it does acknowledge that each has some of both. *Acceptance* is the idea that each individual on a team has absolute value and worth, regardless of who they are or what they are doing. It is the recognition that the individual's current behaviors make sense to him, that he is engaging in them for some reason(s), even if we cannot see, understand, or appreciate those reasons ourselves. It is the further recognition that the individual has the right and freedom to make choices and engage in any behaviors, even those we do not agree with, despite the potential for negative consequences. Acceptance refers to seeking to understand the other individual's situation, to try to "see the world through his eyes," rather than to judge or label him for his beliefs and behaviors. *Compassion* is about promoting the welfare of the individual in front of us, ensuring that we are actively working toward a goal that is in her best interest. The individual practicing MI need not disregard his own best interests, but he certainly does not put these ahead of the other individual(s). Finally, *evocation* is the active and deliberate process of seeking and appreciating the ideas, reasons, and values around change from the other individual. It is the recognition that these ideas have real value and merit, as they are more likely to be compelling to the other person than our own ideas would be, even if we perceive our own ideas to be superior.

It is worth noting that each of the above components of the MI spirit is *necessary* to the practice of MI. That is, if you are unable to honor, promote, or practice each of these components, then you are not engaging in MI. Even with the implementation of the MI roadmap (or processes) and skills we will discuss shortly, without the spirit, you are not practicing MI. Later, we will discuss how to continue to practice transformational leadership in situations where you are unable to honor every aspect of the MI spirit (for example, the individual you are leading has no say in the decision you are about to make; that is, you cannot honestly evoke ideas from him or make him an active partner in the process).

Ambivalence

Another helpful concept needed to truly understand the practice of MI and why it is so effective is *ambivalence*. Ambivalence is feeling two ways about something. It is both wanting and not wanting. When it comes to change, it is recognizing and seeing value in both the pros and cons of changing and of not changing. Ambivalence is a normal and natural part of the change process for human beings. Indeed, many, if not all, of us have experienced ambivalence around some change or another, including change that was important or even necessary for our overall health (for example, eating healthier, exercising more, or quitting smoking). Thus, from the MI perspective, ambivalence is not viewed as a "bad thing" that necessitates punishment or even indifference. Indeed, ambivalence is to be appreciated, if not outright celebrated. It is a sign that change is being considered; that it holds some merit within the individual. Ambivalence could even be a harbinger of change. Within an MI approach, ambivalence is viewed as valuable and worthy of exploration.

How we treat ambivalence is key. Take a moment and consider how you might react to someone telling you that you had to change a behavior that you are ambivalent about. Say your doctor tells you that you must eliminate a certain food from your diet in order to improve your health and avoid certain consequences. For instance, she recommends that you stop consuming coffee because you are developing hypertension. You realize that, in this case, coffee is not particularly good for you, and at the same time, you enjoy it tremendously. After all, it's a fundamental part of your morning routine, it gets you going, and you love the taste! How might you react to your doctor's advice to eliminate it? Would you give in? Argue? Bargain? Get defensive? Be confused? Maybe say you'll do it without any real intent to do so? Many of us in this type of situation, when we're truly ambivalent, will think about, if not outright openly discuss, the many reasons for continuing to drink coffee and/or the many reasons against eliminating it. When your doctor argues for one side of change, she has invited you to consider, and potentially discuss, the value of the other side. It is almost as if the doctor has disturbed your balance between change and not change, and your response is to restore this balance by arguing for the opposite side.

What's really interesting in this process is that whichever side of change we argue for is the side we tend to pursue. Research in this area is clear. When discussing change with an individual, the more the individual argues for personal change, the more likely she is to change, and the more she argues against personal change, the less likely she is to follow through with that change (Miller, Benefield, & Tonigan, 1993; Amrhein, Miller, Yahne, Palmer, & Fulcher, 2003). Think about that for a moment. In the above example, by arguing for eliminating coffee, your doctor may be inadvertently making you *less likely* to do so, despite you both recognizing that limiting caffeine is in your best interest.

In thinking about how we respond to pressure to change during ambivalence, our co-author Dr. Kersh reflects upon a conversation with a friend:

I'm reminded of a recent conversation with a friend who told me he had been considering a move to another state. I became excited about this news because the move would not only bring him and his family closer to where I live, but the area he was considering was a place where my family and I frequently visit because we have family members who live there. This meant that I would get to visit my friend much more frequently than I had in recent years. In my excitement upon hearing this news, I failed to recognize that my friend was still ambivalent about the move. Instead, I immediately began helping him plan the move, including suggesting the route he should travel when moving (so that he and his family could visit with us en route and have a place to stay overnight). His response was to say that he wasn't sure they actually would be moving because of the significant expense involved. In an attempt to be supportive of this potential decision, I stated that he was definitely right to take this into consideration and pointed out that the area where he was thinking about moving had a significantly higher cost of living than where he was currently living. His response to this was to tell me how much he disliked where he was currently living and how he couldn't wait to get out. In essence, my friend was ambivalent about moving. When I attempted to push him toward moving, his response was to tell me why he would be better off not moving. When I agreed with his reasoning for not moving and offered additional information to support that reasoning, his response was tell me more about why he wanted to move. Thus, whichever side I pushed for, he pushed for the other. This is the hallmark of ambivalence.

This important aspect of human nature is useful to understand, especially if we want to more effectively lead individuals and assist them in changing their behavior. If we recognize that the individual is ambivalent, it becomes important to avoid becoming the voice of change and eliciting the voice of status quo from the individual, since this talk about the benefits of maintaining status quo makes him less likely to change. With MI, the goal is to enhance the likelihood that the other person will become the voice of change, thus increasing the probability of change. That is, when practicing MI, we want the other individual to talk more about change (*change talk*) and less about staying the same (*sustain talk*).

Change Talk

What exactly is change talk? Simply put, change talk is any talk that favors movement in the direction of change. We currently recognize seven categories of change talk statements, which are collectively known by the acronym *DARN CAT*, for Desire, Ability, Reason, Need, Commitment, Activating, and Taking Steps. The DARN part of the acronym is referred to as *preparatory language* or language that indicates that someone is preparing to make a change. Specifically, *desire* statements are those indicating a wish for change (for example, "I really want to quit smoking"). Statements of *ability* reflect the individual's capability of making a particular change (for example, "I could figure out a way to get to work on time if I put my mind to it"). *Reason* statements are those that indicate the individual's rationale for changing (for example, "If I use disinfectant in my stored water to keep it clean, my children won't get sick."). *Need* statements are similar to reason statements, although they do not explicitly include the reason for making the change, only that the change should occur (for example, "I really need to avoid violating parole").

The *CAT* part of the acronym is referred to as *mobilizing language* or language that someone uses when they've gotten a little bit closer to making the change or have already started. *Commitment language* indicates a commitment to change (for example, "I will get this project done by the deadline"). *Activating language* is similar to commitment language, although reflects more of a readiness to change than an actual vow to do so (for example, "I'm considering joining a gym"). Finally, statements of *taking steps* are those that indicate *recent* changes that the individual has made around the target behavior ("I arrived at work on time every day last week").

We highlight these seven categories of change talk, not because it is especially important that you identify the category, but rather so that you can recognize change talk in its many different forms. Any and all change talk predicts change, whether it is the individual saying "I could exercise a little more" or "I promise I will go to the gym every day next week." All change talk predicts change, and there is little evidence to suggest that one particular type of change talk is more predictive of change than any other. Thus, it is important to listen for and recognize change talk, whatever shape it may take. And because change talk predicts change, we'll want to do more than just listen for it; we'll also want to actively elicit it from the other person.

Sustain Talk

The opposite of change talk is sustain talk. Sustain talk is any talk that favors the status quo (that is, staying the same). As indicated above, just as change talk predicts change, sustain talk predicts staying the same. If we wish to help the other individual engage in change, we'll want to diminish sustain talk as much as possible, and even guide the discussion in a different direction if we hear significant sustain talk. Therefore, recognizing sustain talk is equally as important as recognizing change talk. So, what does the language of status quo sound like? It turns out that it sounds a lot like *DARN CAT* for staying the same ("I don't want to quit smoking," "There's no way I can get to work on time," "I don't need to disinfect my water," "I won't get this project done on time," "I'm not even considering exercise at this point, much less joining a gym," etc.).

How we respond to sustain talk is especially important. If our response encourages more sustain talk, we are making change even less likely to happen. For example, if my colleague says "I just can't seem to get to work on time," and my response is to ask him to elaborate ("Tell me more about that.") or to reflect ("Mornings are a struggle for you."), then he is likely to engage in more sustain talk (for example, "Well, I'm not a morning person to begin with, and, on top of that, I have to get the kids ready, get them to school, and then battle traffic on the way to work."). Instead, our goal is to diminish sustain talk and set the stage for change talk.

MI Processes

So, how do we get the individual to engage in change talk? First, it is helpful to map out a plan to get there. Within MI, the roadmap to change is described by the *4 Processes*: Engaging, Focusing, Evoking, and Planning. These aren't necessarily discrete stages in MI as they may overlap, and you may not progress through them linearly. Instead, you need to be mindful of where the person you are working with is and where he needs to go. *Engaging* is often the initial process in MI; in it you are building a relationship with the individual with whom you are working. Once a mutually trusting and respectful relationship is in place, the next process is *focusing*, which is mutually agreeing upon a target behavior, or set of behaviors, to consider changing. After the target is established, *evoking* is the process of listening for, eliciting, and strengthening change talk about the target behavior(s). The final process, *planning,* involves discussing the actual steps to implementing change.

As an illustration of the MI processes in action, let us consider a primary care visit where a doctor is talking to one of her patients about improving his health. The doctor *engages* her patient by asking him about a personally relevant topic (for example, "How did that ski trip go?"), inquiring about what he has been doing since the last visit, and then listening closely to and commenting on her patient's responses. She then *focuses* the discussion by asking her patient what he wants to address during the visit, including giving him a few options that she thinks might be helpful to focus on given her review of his current health status. Once they have mutually agreed upon a target, let us say eating healthier, the doctor begins to *evoke* change talk about eating healthier from her patient by asking him *his* reasons and ideas around eating healthier. She might even probe the patient for past attempts around eating healthier and reflect back to the patient any strengths and/or successes she hears. Once it sounds like the patient is ready to make changes around eating healthier, then and only then would the doctor negotiate with her patient an actual *plan* (for example, specific diet or meal plan) for implementing dietary changes.

How does the doctor know that her patient may be ready to make changes and therefore attempt to transition into planning? If her patient is primarily engaging in change talk around eating healthier and engaging in very little, if any, sustain talk, she can be reasonably assured that her patient is ready for planning. She might transition into planning by summarizing the patient's current reasons and past successes around eating healthier and then asking the patient his ideas about moving forward with similar behavior change at this time. If the patient is ready for planning, he will let her know by engaging in the development of the plan, including problem solving with her around any potential barriers. If the patient is not really ready to develop and implement a plan, he will also let her know, this time by resisting, arguing, and/or disengaging around the planning process. In this case, being consistent with the MI spirit, the doctor recognizes that the patient is not ready for change, and returns to one of the prior processes, such as evoking (if the patient remains ambivalent about eating healthier), focusing (if the patient does not really want to work on eating healthier at this time), or engaging (if the relationship deteriorated in the process of working on eating healthier and needs to be re-established). Progression through the MI processes can be a linear course, or it may involve returning to previous processes, especially if we get too far ahead of the other person (for example, we try to work on a plan before engaging with the person or coming to an agreement with that individual as to what behavior to work on changing). If we are willing to listen carefully to others, they will let us know when they are ready to transition to each process, and it is up to us to "meet them where they're at."

OARS

A common set of skills is used throughout each of the four MI processes. These skills are collectively known by the acronym *OARS*, for Open-ended questions, Affirmations, Reflective listening, and Summaries. *Open-ended questions* are those that cannot be answered appropriately with a one-word response, such as *yes, no, 42*, or *Albuquerque*. Instead, open-ended questions invite elaboration. They uphold the spirit of MI by giving the interviewee more latitude in her response. They are more collaborative, evocative, and accepting (by honoring the other individual's autonomy and giving her more freedom) than closed-ended questions. Instead of asking "Did you meet your goals for this week?" you might instead ask, "How are you doing with regard to your goals this week?".

Affirmations are used to recognize strengths, efforts, intentions, and successes. They can honor each and every component of the MI spirit. Affirmations can convey *acceptance* by highlighting the individual's value and worth, regardless of his current behavior. For instance, despite the other's failure to complete a project on time, you might highlight his effort by stating, "You gave it your all."
Affirmations can be *compassionate* as they promote the welfare of the other and serve to build his confidence. Affirmations can also be *evocative*, as they tend to elicit more discussion around the aspect of the individual that was affirmed. Finally, if used appropriately, affirmations can also promote *partnership*. To understand this more fully, it is important to note that affirmations are not the same as praise, which puts at least part of the emphasis on the individual offering praise and could serve to highlight the power differential.

Consider the difference between someone telling you, "I like how you did that" versus, "You put a lot of effort into that." The first statement carries an implication that it was good that you pleased the speaker. The second merely highlights the effort you put into the task, without bringing the speaker into it. This is a subtle distinction, and it can also be a powerful one. As a general rule of thumb, when offering affirmations, as much as possible make the other person the focus of the statement and leave yourself out of it.

Reflective listening is the cornerstone of MI. It is the single most important skill when it comes to fostering change in others. Reflective listening is the process of listening carefully to what the other person is saying, as well as *how* they are saying it (by also attuning to tone and volume of speech, as well as body language), and then offering back what was said in the form of a statement. Reflections can be simple and stick to the content of what the individual said without going beyond the surface. Reflections can also be complex and highlight the underlying meaning of or emotion behind what was said. If an individual says, "It's too hard for me to exercise right now. There's just not enough time in the day," a simple reflection might be, "You don't have time to exercise more right now." A simple reflection rephrases the speaker's words and does not go beyond the surface of what the speaker said. A more complex reflection would be, "You'd really like to exercise more if you could find the time," or "Exercise isn't your top priority right now," or "You're frustrated that you cannot exercise more." All three of these statements go below the surface of what was said, by offering unmentioned concepts like desire, priorities, or underlying emotion, respectively. Both simple and complex reflections are useful and have their place, although complex reflections can be more effective and efficient at guiding the discussion toward change.

So, what's the point of reflecting? Again, it goes back to the MI spirit. Reflections are collaborative, as they give the speaker incredible latitude in his/her response. They also allow the speaker more input into the agenda of the conversation, unlike questions, in which the asker more clearly defines the agenda. Reflections are accepting as they do not offer judgment as to what was said. Quite the opposite, reflections validate what was said. Reflections are also evocative as they encourage more elaboration from the speaker. Indeed, they tend to elicit elaboration of change talk, more so even than open-ended questions, when used effectively.

The last of the fundamental MI skill is *summaries*. Summaries are a series of reflections strung together. They honor the MI spirit in much the same way as reflections – they can be used to request additional elaboration (for example, "You said you'd like to quit smoking in order to breathe easier, save money, and gain more energy. What else?"), transition from one MI process to another (for example, transition from evoking to planning), or transition from one topic to another (for example, move from discussing documentation to time management).

As noted above, each of these skills is used throughout all four MI processes. In the coming chapters, we'll discuss how the goal and function of these skills vary across the processes, and how the MI spirit, processes, and skills apply more directly to transformational leadership. We'll also further examine the role of ambivalence, the *righting reflex* (a common but ineffective response to ambivalence), and sustain and change talk in transformational leadership.

Chapter Summary

Before we move on to these topics, let's briefly review the general MI framework we have discussed in this chapter. MI is about promoting change by eliciting an individual's own motivation to change. It does this first and foremost by emphasizing a certain spirit or way of being with others that focuses on partnership, acceptance, compassion, and evocation. MI recognizes that ambivalence is a normal part of the change process and that, when an individual is ambivalent about change, the more an outside agent tries to push the individual toward change, the more the individual pushes back, which makes change less likely to occur. The goal of MI, then, is to get the individual to engage more in talk about change (that is, *change talk*), which makes change more likely to happen, and to engage in less talk about staying the same (that is, *sustain talk*). The roadmap to change is laid out in the MI processes, which involve engaging with the individual, mutually agreeing upon a focus for change, evoking discussion around change, and finally mapping out an actual change plan. The skills used within each of these processes are asking open-ended questions, offering affirmations, reflective listening, and summarizing.

Now that we better understand the general MI framework, let's discuss how to apply this framework to leadership. In the next chapter, we'll provide a poignant example of the application of MI in transformational leadership. In so doing, we hope to illustrate one of many types of situations where MI-Lead can be effective and how this approach can develop trust, positive relationships, and improved team engagement, the very components noted in our first chapter to increase individual satisfaction, decrease turnover, and improve organizational functioning.

Chapter 3

Why MI-Lead

Leadership at its essence is connecting with others while guiding in a particular direction. One movie that demonstrates this point is *Concussion (2015)* starring Will Smith. The movie is about a pathologist who discovers the brain damage occurring to football players when they are concussed from repeated hits to the head.

When the pathologist, who is played by Will Smith, announces and publishes his findings, it angers a lot of people, as they see him as an attacker trying to ruin the game they love (of course, in the storyline, the football industry's slandering of the doctor doesn't help). In the movie, he starts out by reporting the science and the facts, and people respond poorly. There is an interesting scene in which Will Smith and Alec Baldwin (playing another doctor) are discussing a presentation that Will Smith's character is preparing to make. Alec's character advises him to make references to football in order to connect with the audience. Will Smith's character appears to struggle with the idea, wanting instead to report the medical findings as hard truths, which ends up disconnecting him from his audience.

However, later in the movie, Will Smith's character takes the other doctor's advice, and he engages the audience. The result is a moving speech in which he begins to use language that connects him with the crowd. What he says resonates with the group and allows them the freedom to really listen to, consider, and eventually accept the information.

MI-Lead works in a similar manner, helping to connect the ideas of leadership with those being led. This is done in a way that honors autonomy and opens the door for others to bring out their thoughts, values, solutions, and goals.

We talked in the last chapter about the idea that people facing any type of change may experience ambivalence and that our attempts to help them resolve that ambivalence through our own suggestions may actually decrease the likelihood of the very changes we are attempting to support. However, in the midst of their different feelings and perspectives, those same individuals have ideas that can move them through roadblocks, and, by eliciting those ideas and solutions from the individuals themselves, we, as leaders, actually increase the likelihood that they will successfully engage in personal and/or system change. MI-Lead provides a framework for leaders to help those being led resolve their ambivalence about change by encouraging them to examine and articulate their own ideas, their thoughts about the importance of a particular behavior or system process, and their confidence in their ability to succeed. Through this approach, those being led identify their own solutions using ideas they already have within.

The success of using the Ml-Lead approach is based upon the fact that human beings are hard-wired to prefer their own ideas over those produced by others. A recent research study (Feldstein Ewing, Yezhuvath, Houck, & Filbey, 2014) looked at activity levels in various parts of the brain using fMRI to compare the differences in brain processing of ideas that were generated from external forces (other people) versus ideas that were generated by the study subjects themselves. Results from the study suggested that ideas provided by others or an exterior source led to increased activity in some areas of the brain but not in those areas that encourage action. In contrast, when the ideas came from within the individual considering change or were self-generated, the part of the brain that influences change became more active. This study sheds a little more light on how MI-Lead may work and provides further evidence that we are more likely to engage in change when we generate the ideas for change ourselves.

This research highlights the physiological mechanisms involved in communication styles that do and do not lead to action. Metaphorically, certain styles of communicating with an individual act like a green light for positive action in the brain, and certain styles of communicating act like a red light for action. In MI terms, motivation for action, or change in behavior, occurs when we utilize a style of communicating that offers gentle guidance while honoring a person's autonomy.

Before further describing how to apply MI in the context of leadership, consider the following scenario that occurred while co-author Jason Wilcox was working with "Mary", an executive leader at a large medical system of approximately 1200 employees. Following her training in MI-Lead, Mary sought Jason's advice, describing a recent encounter with an employee. The following conversation transpired:

"So tell me what's going on?" Jason asked.

"Ok, so, I have this employee who is leading a team to find a solution to a problem we are having in our system," Mary explained.

"She had thought that once they identified the solution, leadership would just adopt their decisions. However, when it was presented to me, it was obvious we couldn't go forward with the idea for multiple reasons."

"What was the major concern?" Jason elicited.

"She wanted to hire a bunch of new staff to run a new program that hadn't yet been developed, a program that had never been tried or tested, and we aren't in a position to hire new staff. Not only was *it a new program that would need new staff, but a lot of their job would just be another layer of oversight that two other departments already do."*

"Oh, I see," Jason listened intently.

"I let it be known that we couldn't support that program, and her immediate supervisor had already explained this to her too." Mary shook her head. "And as you might imagine, the next thing I knew, the employee was in my office, and she was telling me that I was ruining their program and nothing was going to work now unless I allowed the program to go forward."

"So she was really upset," Jason reflected.

"Oh yes." Mary said with a sigh. "I tried to tell her that we couldn't afford to just start hiring people to fill these new positions. I told her to go back and come up with a way to pilot the program so we could at least test it, but that didn't work. She just kept telling me I was killing their work and there was nothing else that could be done to fix the problem. She's a smart employee, Jason, so I really tried to help her see she just needed to show that the idea would work and that a pilot would be a great opportunity to gather some information."

"She really didn't like your idea of starting out with a pilot."

"No, she hated my idea." Mary added, "At the end she said, 'You're the leader, so I guess we'll just have to do what you say,' and then she left."

"From your perspective, you felt this didn't go well at all."

"No, it was surprising."

After Mary finished explaining, she and Jason reviewed some specific concepts like the spirit of MI-Lead, open-ended questions, reflections, etc., and then role-played a follow up conversation incorporating MI-Lead techniques. Mary then decided that she would go back to the employee that week and try the skills in a follow-up conversation.

Unfortunately, the follow-up conversation didn't happen that week. When Mary approached the employee, the employee quickly responded that she was unwilling to talk unless the entire group was present. Consistent with the MI processes, Mary recognized that this employee was not ready to willingly engage in a discussion about the pilot project with her, and she honored this request and moved on. At this point, pushing the employee to engage in further discussion about the topic would potentially jeopardize their relationship, which Mary recognized was a priority.

A few days later the team met together with Mary, and Mary took this opportunity to try her new MI-Lead skills. After the meeting, Jason received this phone call:

"Hello, Mary." Jason answered the phone.

"You are going to be so impressed." Mary's voice was full of excitement.

"What's going on?"

"I just had the meeting today with the employee I was telling you about, along with the rest of her group, and the MI-Lead worked. It really worked!" Her excitement was still bubbling through the phone.

"That's great!" Jason responded. *"Tell me about it."*

"So, I went in to the meeting and did just like we practiced and started out with an open-ended question. That really opened the conversation and for the most part I didn't really have to say much. I just kept using the principles we went over. Instead of offering advice, I tried to stay curious about their ideas for solutions. Then I reflected back the ideas they came up with. And I'll tell you what, there was a huge difference with the outcome of this meeting versus

the last meeting we had. It was like, the more I listened and just reflected back what I heard, the more ideas they came up with! Even that employee I told you about that got so upset and said she didn't want to do the pilot was coming up with ideas."

"Really? It sounds like she reacted very differently this time" Jason, of course, was pleased to hear the outcome.

"Exactly! Not only by the end did she agree to do the pilot, but she was actually excited about it and couldn't wait to get going on it. I'm telling you, it was a night and day difference. Instead of being upset and unwilling to talk, she opened up and was willing to brainstorm on lots of options."

"What do you think changed for her?"

Mary paused a moment and then replied, " I think it was because I was different. I was able to show her that I was really interested in hearing the team's ideas, and I was really surprised at how many good ideas they really had. I didn't have to give them any of my suggestions because they came up with most of them anyway!"

As the example demonstrates, Mary's change in her communication style and approach with her employees made a significant difference. By focusing on listening, evoking ideas from the others at the table, and reflecting those ideas back to her employees, Mary left the interaction with a much more engaged and motivated team.

This is just one example that really highlights how effective MI-Lead can be when used by those in a leadership position. Mary was ecstatic about the results she experienced first-hand. It was obvious that it brought back some of the enthusiasm that she had when she first became a leader. Not only did the employee leave the interaction feeling heard and that her ideas were valued, but Mary also benefitted, finding herself better able to address the discord that had arisen, to engage the team in a collaborative manner, and to support the employees' efforts to develop new and innovative ideas that could benefit the hospital itself. As illustrated here, MI-Lead benefits all members of the team when used effectively.

Mary's story doesn't end with her successful interaction with her employee. As a result of this successful interaction, Mary began to shift her overall communication style as a leader. She summarized her thoughts to Jason a short time later, *"I've known what MI is and have used it in the medical setting with patients. I love MI. It works great, but I'll have to admit, I had never thought about using it as a leader. It just never occurred to me. But now that I have, it makes so much sense. In fact, I don't know why all leaders don't use MI. It really works."*

This is a theme we have heard time and time again in our work with leaders, and this is what inspired us to share this book. MI is a way of being with people that addresses ambivalence and supports individuals as they make decisions about engaging in particular behavior changes. As we present this book and examine the different components that make up MI-Lead, we hope you will experience the same success and excitement that Mary did. MI-Lead can be a very powerful communication style when used correctly. As we describe in more detail later, the MI-Lead approach is not intended to manipulate others. Instead, it is designed to help leaders guide and work collaboratively with others in a manner that helps promote both individual and team goals.

In the rest of this book we will present the specific concepts of MI-Lead that Mary learned and provide exercises for you to practice as you develop your own skills. We suggest that, as you are reading, you pause and consider how the concepts may be relevant in your work. Research has shown that even shifting your approach to be a little more consistent with MI can have a pronounced positive impact on the behavior of the individual with whom you are working (Pollak, 2010).

Chapter 4

Spirit of MI

Let's continue our exploration of MI-Lead by further discussing the *spirit* of MI, the very foundation of both MI and MI-Lead. Without this foundation, which is present throughout all the processes, skills, and techniques, you aren't actually using MI-Lead. Think of the spirit of MI as a top hat that you choose to wear when discussing change with others. When you wear your top hat, you are interacting with the individual or system in a way that is collaborative, respectful and supportive of the individual or system even if it's perspective is not the same as your own, actively trying to understand this perspective especially when it differs from yours, and being curious and evoking. Your MI hat includes an approach that emphasizes partnership, acceptance, compassion, and evocation.

Consider an example that contrasts this spirit with a more self-serving approach to interacting with others. Jason Wilcox once worked as a car salesman, and he was grateful it was for only a brief time. There were several very successful salespeople at the car dealership. One day while sitting down with these salespeople, Jason explained that his brother was coming in to buy a car and that he was excited because he wanted to get a great deal for his brother, with whom he was close. While other salespeople were also excited for Jason, their reasons were different from his. They expressed excitement that Jason might be able to profit monetarily by taking advantage of his family's trust in him.

While this desire to capitalize on the goodwill of family is not necessarily representative of all salespeople, several sales staff where Jason worked did express a motive to make as much money as possible from everyone, even if it meant taking advantage of the trust of friends, family, or any customer that came to the store. While these staff may have used some of the tools we use in MI, such as open-ended questions and affirmations, they used them in a way that was self-focused, manipulative, and disrespectful of the desires and needs of others. This is in direct contrast with the spirit of MI. These salespeople did not wear their MI hats.

MI-Lead does not employ manipulation, bulldozing, or micromanaging. Instead of demanding or forcing someone to change, engage, or do something, it emphasizes collaboration, acceptance, empathy, and an eliciting style to support an individual as he or she determines what will be consistent with his or her values and goals. Many have described this coaching style as gentle guidance, much like dancing with a partner.

Partnership is fundamental to the MI spirit. Imagine the difference between sitting in front of someone who is in a position of authority over you and sitting next to that same person. When you wear your MI hat, you tend to work side by side with those that you lead, much as a coach guides a learner who is adopting new skills. You approach the potential for change as a partner who is co-exploring new possibilities. While you may have a great deal of expertise about some of these possibilities, the individual or system with whom you are working brings expertise to the table as well. The individual knows what has been tried in the past, what has been effective or ineffective, what has supported previous change, and what the values or rationale underlying the commitment to change may be. When you wear your MI hat, you remember that there are multiple "experts" in the room.

Acceptance is another key component of the MI spirit. It involves implicitly and explicitly communicating our appreciation of an individual's worthwhile actively attempting to understand the person's perspective. The ability to understand an individual's perspective, whether or not it is consistent with our own, is called accurate empathy. It requires checking our own assumptions at the door. Empathy is not hearing with the goal of responding; it is listening with the goal of understanding. Acceptance also involves honoring an individual's autonomy to make decisions, in spite of the fact that the perspective and related choices may differ from our own. While respecting an individual's autonomy doesn't mean there won't be consequences to their choices that are in contrast with any policies or rules, it does mean that we can honor the importance of choice. Finally, acceptance also involves affirming an individual's own ability to find solutions. It requires that we as leaders "trust the process" by focusing upon the capacity of others to succeed, by identifying and affirming an individual's strengths and resources for change.

Often when we give feedback it may be perceived as judgmental in tone, and it may take some practice to shift the tone to a more accepting one. The comments we make that are based from our personal beliefs about what is right or wrong, good or bad, black or white, are frequently perceived as statements of judgment, even when positive. Judgmental comments are one of the fastest ways to shut down a conversation with anyone and often shut down motivation, engagement, and creativity. Often, shifting the feedback to data-based statements versus value-based statements will serve the same informative purposes without jeopardizing the engagement between leaders and led.

While an individual such as Jason's fellow car salesman may understand the perspective of another, that understanding must be accompanied by *Compassion* in order for it to be consistent with the spirit of MI. Without compassion, that information about what motivates another can be used in a self-serving manner. Compassion involves prioritizing the needs of an individual without blame or judgment. The focus is on promoting the individual's welfare.

Lastly, the spirit of MI is *Evoking*. You as the leader remain interested in and curious about the individual's experience, reasons for change, confidence in making change happen, and readiness for that change. When we wear our MI hats, we seek out information from individuals about their ideas, goals, and values. An evoking style elicits information about the "what", "why", "how", and "when" from the individual instead of imparting that information onto that person. An evoking style involves more listening and less talking. The success of this style is based upon our understanding that the desire, ability, reasons, and need for change come from within and from our awareness that a "telling" or more directive style is likely to elicit arguments against change, which translate into a decreased likelihood for change.

When we see someone struggle, it can be tempting to try to help solve that problem, or "make it right" by immediately "fixing" it or by making suggestions. This desire to "make it right" is referred to as the *Righting Reflex,* and it is a potential barrier to respecting the autonomy, or perspectives, of those we lead. When we see something "wrong" and we feel pulled to use our expertise to "just fix it", we are being tempted by the righting reflex. Think of that strong desire when you are sitting in the passenger's seat while someone else is driving and they start making driving mistakes. Your instincts or righting reflex quickly kicks in as you want to tell the person how to drive and what they could've done better. Perhaps you've watched your child as she learned a new skill and felt that pull to jump in and "do it for" her. That knee-jerk desire to fix, correct, or direct another person's behavior is the righting reflex.

How does this relate to being a leader? Imagine that you are talking with a supervisee named Steven who is struggling to work effectively with his colleague Jacob, because Jacob tends to be overly aggressive and pushy. Immediately, you may have some ideas for how to resolve the problem. You may tell Steven how to "fix it" in an attempt to help. While this reflex to immediately offer suggestions is well intentioned, that's your righting reflex, alive and well, kicking in to "fix" the situation.

How might the "fixing" that occurs with the righting reflex be problematic? After all, it generally comes from a genuine desire to help. However, by telling someone what to do and how to do it, you assume the role of "expert", and the relationship ceases to be one of collaboration. If your goal is to support Steven in assuming a greater degree of responsibility and sense of ownership for his decisions and his work, then your role will need to be that of a coach versus that of the expert. When you assume the role of the advice-wielding expert, it is human nature for the other person to argue the other side, and your attempts to provide solutions may, in fact, have the opposite effect. Your solutions may elicit arguments against change, known as sustain talk, or even a deterioration in the relationship (that is, discord). Your solutions are likely to encourage Steven to find reasons to argue against the ideas and why they won't work.

Steven's reaction is human nature, and research shows us that this argument against your ideas for change, or for the status quo, actually serves to decrease Steven's motivation to engage in your suggested solutions. His arguments against your advice decrease the likelihood that he will eventually engage in this new approach. Recalling the earlier example, when Dr. Kersh provided his friend with well-intentioned advice about whether or not to move, his friend responded with arguments against each recommendation that Dr. Kersh provided. His friend was reacting to the righting reflex the way most of us tend to do when we feel pushed to do things in a certain way. We react in a way that emphasizes our desire to maintain a sense of autonomy or freedom to make our own choices.

In leadership, there is another important consideration with regards to the righting reflex. There is an inherent power differential that exists between leaders and those they lead. This gap in power increases further when a leader's righting reflex is in play. As this gap increases, it tends to decrease a sense of ownership for the end results and prevent someone in Steven's shoes from reaching his or her maximum potential. In contrast, when individuals feel like they are an integral part of the creative process, that their input into the development of new systems, programs, plans, materials, etc. is worthwhile, and that their ideas and solutions to challenges are sought after and valued, the importance they place on quality and their confidence in their ability to make a difference will increase.

In summary, the MI spirit involves *Partnership, Acceptance, Compassion,* and *Evocation.* Many times, those we work with do not share our vision or reasons for engaging in a particular behavior or changing a particular approach. These differences in perspective can be hard to accept, and, yet, consider the alternative. Without acceptance of individual's autonomy, we may feel compelled to "push" our vision of "what", "why", or "how" things "should be done", and we may inadvertently decrease the likelihood that an individual will make desired changes. The spirit of MI-Lead is to work in collaboration with the individuals we lead, to maintain a commitment to their well-being, and to honor their autonomy, or in other words, to accept and respect that others have the right to make choices. The approach is one of being <u>curious</u> that involves eliciting reasons, goals, values, ideas, and solutions from those we lead.

Miller and others have described the spirit of MI as being analogous to dancing versus wrestling, or guiding and collaborating versus pushing. Similarly, in a flowing river, when we swim against the current, the current continues to push us back; alternatively, if we swim with the current, we are better able to guide our general direction. The spirit of MI works in a similar way. When you are honoring that spirit, you will feel that you are moving with the current rather than against it. Conversations will flow more smoothly and have limited or no discord or push back.

When leadership authority is used to enforce a change in another's behavior, it may be successful, temporarily. However, this enforcement comes with a potential cost. The threat of negative consequences as a means for controlling behavior is in direct contrast with the spirit of MI. It does not respect an individual's autonomy. Instead, it increases the power differential between leader and led, decreases the other person's trust and initiative, and may create push back. This push back is known as discord. While there are times when leadership authority must be utilized to ensure a particular outcome, it is important to maintain an awareness that it can be counterproductive when maintaining others' engagement or motivation to work on goals or action plans. Guiding someone using MI-Lead tends to be more effective in helping others achieve their goals both short term and long term when compared with authoritarian control.

Now, the spirit of MI shouldn't be confused with passiveness. Let's consider an example. A manager, Jennifer, had two employees that were fighting and having conduct issues. Jennifer was very passive in the situation, worried that she would cause more problems if she did anything, so she did nothing. This passive approach to managing her employees only made things worse as it made it difficult for the team to meet goals, and the negativity spread. MI-Lead is directive in that it remains focused on the best interest of others and on specific goals for an individual that may align with the leader's and organization's goals. In addition, this passive approach to leadership was inconsistent with the spirit of MI. Giving feedback about desired goals is important for effective leadership, and having clear and collaborative discussions with those that you lead about action plans, outcomes, barriers, and potential changes while respecting others needs is consistent with the spirit of MI. We'll cover more in a future chapter about giving feedback in an MI-Lead consistent way.

In the following chapter, we will delve more extensively into specific skills that can support the spirit of MI. Over the next few pages you will find activities to help you become better at adopting the spirit of MI.

Activity 4.1

Try to take time over the next day or two and see if you can identify any judgmental, righting reflex, prescriptive, pushing, etc., comments in your dialogue with others. Don't get too caught up in getting rid of them yet, just see if you can start catching them and being aware of them. As you become more comfortable with catching yourself in these areas, take the next steps by trying to keep the spirit of MI.

Activity 4.2

Over the next week if someone that you lead comes to you about an issue they are facing, try to actively listen without using the righting reflex. Write insights and thoughts on a piece of paper on what went well and what could've gone even better.

Activity 4.3

In the below leadership and supervisory situations, see if you can identify which responses are consistent with the spirit of MI, which are inconsistent with the spirit of MI, and which are specific examples of the righting reflex. Answers are given at the end. For any that aren't MI-Lead consistent, see if you can come up with a more MI-Lead consistent response.

1. **Team Member**: Today has been a very difficult day because everyone I call won't listen to what I have to tell them. They just hang up on me.

    Leader: Sounds like we need to work on what you are saying. You might want to start out by asking how their day is going.

2. **Team Member**: I don't have any more time in my schedule to add another project.

Leader: I'm not asking if you have time, just make it happen.

3. **Team Member**: I may be late on the due date of my project because of some new issues that have popped up.

    Leader: Tell me a little more about what's going on so I get a clearer picture.

4. **Employee**: I've made 3 sales already this morning.

    Supervisor: John has already made 8 because he wasn't wasting time talking in-between calls.

5. **Employee**: I've run into a few problems installing the software on the new system. I'm not sure if the software is compatible.

    Supervisor: It is compatible. You just need to turn off the firewall first.

6. **Employee**: I keep having a problem cutting the old line and installing the new one.

    Supervisor: If it's all right with you, let's go ahead and have you show me what you've been doing so I can get a better feel for what you are facing.

Activity 4.3 Answers

1. *Righting Reflex*. Example of an MI consistent response: "Sounds like you're having a hard day. I wonder what I might do to help."

2. *Inconsistent*. Example of an MI consistent response: "Sounds like your schedule is completely filled, and you don't see where you can fit another thing in."

3. *Consistent*.

4. *Inconsistent*. Example of an MI consistent response: "You worked hard to get those 3 sales today and you feel good about them."

5. *Righting Reflex*. Example of an MI consistent response: "You're not sure we're running the right software. What do we need to do to make sure everything's in order?"

6. *Consistent*.

Chapter 5

Four Processes in MI

If you have ever worked in sales, you will probably agree that there are more factors involved in a successful sale than simply pushing your product. A successful sale first requires that the seller develop a positive relationship with the buyer, one which includes trust. Secondly, the seller will often find out what is important to the buyer. Thirdly, the seller will engage the individual in a discussion about the product, what makes it important, and how it will bring something desirable to the buyer. Generally, a successful seller tailors this discussion around what is important to the buyer. Finally, when the buyer has decided to purchase the product, the buyer and seller work out the details or plan for that purchase.

Now consider what will likely happen if a step is introduced prematurely or even skipped during the sales process. Many of us have had the displeasure of visiting a car lot with the goal of casually looking at the various cars available only to feel pounced upon by a circling dealer who quickly begins telling us what we should buy and why, without considering our input or goals. This tactic of pushing too quickly through steps 1 and 2 to steps 3 or even 4 of the buying process tends to be off-putting to the buyer and generally does not facilitate the sale. Without some degree of trust of the seller and a subsequent discussion about what is important to the buyer, the sale will likely fail.

While MI is NOT about selling a product, its success in facilitating individual or organizational change depends on four similar processes: engaging, focusing, evoking change talk, and planning. In MI, we start by 1) building a relationship with an individual or team, 2) then establishing a focus for individual or organizational change, 3) followed by encouraging an individual or a team to talk about the focus/target behavior, including their reasons for, ability around, and commitment to making the targeted change, and, 4) potentially, their plans for engaging in the change. The core MI skills, asking open-ended questions, affirming, reflecting, and summarizing (OARS), are important tools throughout each of these processes, although the purpose of these skills will differ among the processes. In this chapter, we'll further explore how these four processes fit into MI-Lead and discuss how some of the OARS are used in each process.

Engaging

Through engaging, you as a leader work to establish a connection with those you lead and to develop a relationship of trust by seeking to understand an individual or team's perspective. This is not a one-time discussion. Instead, it is a style of interacting on a continuous basis with each person or group, in which you demonstrate curiosity and respect for the individual's goals, values, ideas, and concerns. Attention is paid to understanding their reality. Engaging includes recognizing and affirming the strengths and motivation of the person or group and accepting without judgment what you learn about them.

"Tell me about you."

"What are your priorities?"

"Where would you like to be three years from now?"

"What are your thoughts about some of the areas we are looking at with this project?"

"Tell me a little bit about you in terms of what you believe is a strength?"

"What are some of the things that you feel are going really well for you?"

"When it comes to your job, what is your passion?"

Focusing

Focusing is a process by which you and those you lead collaboratively determine a direction for the conversation, specifically focused on a discussion about a specific individual or organizational change. It involves setting a shared agenda and establishing a collaborative, strategic focus. While focusing, you, the leader, explore, without judgment, the person or team's feelings about engaging in a behavior or a change, with attention to deepening your understanding of their motivation and factors underlying that motivation. During this process, both you and those you lead may share information that can be useful in developing the shared, strategic focus.

Questions often heard during focusing might include:

"What are your concerns today?"

"What do you feel is most important for us to address during our meeting?"

"Where would you like to begin?"

"If you were to change something about [area of concern], what might that be?"

"What would the needed change look like to you? And how might we go about getting there?"

During focusing, the leader may choose to share information or make recommendations. Recalling the spirit of MI-Lead, the tone is collaborative. Providing information begins with an assessment of the individual or team's existing understanding about the behavior, situation, or change needed. It continues with the leader showing respect for the individual's or the team's autonomy by asking if it's okay to share information.

"What is your understanding of _____?"

"What has your experience with _____ been? What have you learned?"

"What would you like to know?"

"If it's alright with you, I'd like to share some ideas that others have found helpful in similar situations."

After assessing their understanding and acquiring permission, the leader provides clear, concise information in third party form, tailored to the individual or team's goals, concerns, and values:

"Some individuals in your situation find that _____ may be helpful."

"Some individuals decide _____."

"There are some options for addressing _____ that some individuals have used successfully in similar situations."

The leader's job is not done after information has been provided. The next step is to assess the team's understanding and thoughts about the information that has been provided. In doing so you are working within the spirit of MI, and emphasizing that the individual or team is ultimately the one who determines whether or not they will make use of the information:

- "What are your thoughts about what we've just discussed?"
- "What do you take away from this discussion?"
- "Which, if any, of these options might work for you?"
- "How does what we discussed fit in with what you were thinking (or already knew)?"
- "How might you .. ?"

This style of sharing information is the *Elicit-Provide-Elicit* (or EPE) format:

Elicit their understanding

Provide information (with permission)

Elicit their thoughts about this information

Evoking Change Talk

Once a strategic focus has been agreed upon, the discussion becomes increasingly focused on eliciting talk about change, about the pros of changing and the downside of not making that change. The presence of change talk is associated with eventual change or engagement in the change process. More change talk means an increased likelihood for change. During evoking, the individual or team is encouraged to look at the desired individual or system change as it compares with the current state. Goals and values are explored as well.

- "How important is this [change] to you on a scale of 0-10?"
- "What helps you know that you could do this?"
- "Why is this important to you?"

- "How does [the current way of doing this] fit with [the desired change]?"

During this process, the individual's or team's ambivalence about engaging in the desired behavior is also addressed using empathic listening, in which the leader seeks to understand the individual's or team's concerns while also supporting their efforts to address barriers that may exist to engaging in the change. Recognizing and responding to change talk with reflections and requests for elaboration is particularly important during this process. Reflections of change talk tend to elicit more change talk, and more change talk is predictive of eventual change.

Planning

As the individual or team moves towards a readiness to engage in a change, the leader will frequently summarize what they have discussed so far and support the individual or team in identifying their own goal or plan for change. An examination of both desire for change (i.e., importance) and confidence (i.e., ability) to successfully engage in a change can be especially valuable. Therefore, your work together will ideally address both of these elements during the planning process. Potential barriers to success are also identified, problem solving is utilized, with solutions being elicited from the individual or team, and a follow-up discussion is arranged.

The first three processes (engaging, focusing, and evoking change talk) are especially important in MI-Lead. If you push towards a plan for resolution before the individual or team have established a sense of trust with you and before they have agreed upon an agenda, your most well-laid plans are likely to fail. Why? Research has shown that the better predictor of change is change talk (i.e., any statements about desire, ability, reasons, need, commitment, readiness, and/or taking steps around change) that comes from the individual or team, not from you the leader. In fact, if someone isn't ready to make the change and you push for it, you are likely to find the person will begin to argue against change. Research shows that the more someone talks about the benefits of the status quo (no change) and the downside of changing, the less likely they are to change. Makes sense!

Imagine a three-legged race, and you and an individual you lead are a team. The two of you must progress through all four processes in order to successfully complete the race. If you, in your enthusiasm, quickly try to finish the race, attempt to reach planning before your partner has finished engaging, focusing, or developing change talk, you have gotten ahead of your teammate, and thus your team is likely to stumble and fall. Collaboration is essential to successfully completing the race.

Similarly, if you find yourself pushing an individual or team to make a change but you sense reluctance in the form of arguments against change or statements for the status quo, it may be helpful to pause in your efforts to convince them, and consider where they are in terms of the MI-Lead processes. Perhaps they are not yet feeling connected or secure in their relationship with you. Or perhaps they trust you but are not in agreement about the longer term goal or identified target behavior. Adjusting your leadership approach to match the person or team's readiness for change will increase the likelihood that they will eventually and successfully engage in the targeted change.

Chapter Summary

To summarize, there are four processes in MI-Lead: engaging, focusing, evoking, and planning. Each process requires that the previous processes be fully addressed. The progress through these processes is not always linear, and leaders may need to frequently step back as change is being discussed to assess where an individual or team is and to adjust the discussion so that the leadership approach matches where the individual or team is in terms of processes. Your approach to the person or team will vary based upon their actual readiness for change.

Chapter 6

MI Core Skills (OARS)

As a leader, you likely have a sense of where your team is in terms of functioning and what you would like them to be achieving. You know that those you lead are unlikely to respond well if you are always telling them what to do. For example, you know your team is likely to respond poorly if you walk into the team meeting and state, "This is the plan that you are going to follow, and this is how I want you to do it."

How you support and guide your team is critical for motivation, action, ownership of the problem, and the decision to engage in a change. This is where the MI-Lead skills come into play.

In previous chapters, we discussed OARS, a straightforward set of skills to help put the MI framework into practice. OARS is an acronym for Open-ended questions, Affirmations, Reflective listening, and Summaries. In this chapter, we discuss each of these skills in greater detail and describe why and how to put them into practice. We'll also include some examples of the use of these skills in leadership settings as well as some exercises to provide you with opportunities to practice doing the same.

Open-Ended Questions

Open-ended questions ask for elaboration and seek more information than their closed-ended brethren, which tend to pull for one-word answers (such as a "yes" or "no" answer, or a date, place, or time). Open-ended questions are effective to use with those you lead because they are collaborative, evocative, and accepting. They provide the avenue for others to open up, as opposed to shutting down or narrowly limiting the length and range of responses. It is true that we sometimes need very specific bits of information from others, such as the location of a particular file or the name of a particular client, and asking closed-ended questions are much more efficient and useful at obtaining this information. But consider the impact of asking a series of closed-ended questions. You are conveying to the other individual that you are in charge, that you are setting the agenda, and that you only want certain pieces of information ("I didn't ask for your life story, just tell me 'yes' or 'no'"). Being on the receiving end of a series of these types of questions can quickly come to feel like an interrogation. If our goal is, instead, to promote change, to enhance creativity, to empower those we lead, or to generate new ideas, then we are better off using open-ended questions.

So how do we ask open-ended questions? Just like that! Starting a question with a word like "how," "why," or "what" will generally make it open-ended, however this is not always the case. Consider the question "How old are you?" (closed-ended because it can be answered with a one word answer) versus "How do you feel about your age?" (open-ended as it invites a more elaborative response). Similarly, starting a question with "what" does not guarantee that it will be open-ended ("What time is it?"). The true determination of whether a question is open-ended is if it invites the other to elaborate. Although not technically a question, starting with "tell me" is considered an open-ended inquiry as it invites the same elaboration ("Tell me your thoughts about the project.").

Closed-ended questions, on the other hand, tend to start with words like "do," "did," "have," "is", "are," "can," "could," "should", "were," or "was." In general, we recommend avoiding asking questions that start with these words, unless you are seeking a very specific, short, information-related response (for example, "Did you get the report submitted on time?"). If you are instead seeking to engage, empower, and/or inspire others, start your questions with "how," "why," or "what" and make sure that you leave room for elaboration in the response (for example, "What ideas do you have about the project?" "How do you propose we go about improving customer satisfaction?" "Why do you think that is?").

Affirmations

Affirmations are statements that acknowledge the other person's strengths, efforts, values, successes, intentions, and/or desires. In other words, they serve to highlight the positive. These simple statements can be powerful, not only by connecting with the person, but also by orienting individuals and groups to their strengths. As human beings, many of us see our weaknesses or areas needing improvement before we look to our strengths. It should be worth noting, however, that people generally do not strive to achieve from a place of worthlessness, lack of confidence, or hopelessness, which can happen when we focus on our weaknesses. Instead, we make an effort when we feel worthy, confident, and hopeful. In short, we try when we think we might succeed. A well-connected affirmation can really empower someone.

So, how do we affirm? Isn't this simply cheerleading? Not quite. The keys to affirming are to be genuine and tailor your statement to an actual behavior or characteristic you perceived in the other individual(s). Affirmations are less "Yay, team" and more "The time and energy you all are putting into this project are really paying off!" Affirmations are also more effective when they are focused on the other individual(s) and leave ourselves out of the equation. For instance, "You really worked hard on that" is more collaborative than "I like that you did that," as the latter might serve to highlight an existing power differential (it is basically implying that I'm the leader and it's good that you pleased me). In general, when using affirmations, we suggest keeping the focus on the other individual(s) by using "you" in the statement and leaving "I" out. Here are some examples:

- "You gave it your all."

- "Your work on fundraising has been incredibly beneficial!"

- "Despite the setbacks, you really stuck with it."

- "Your dedication to this project has really paid off!"

- "The work you did on employee training had a big impact on our customer satisfaction ratings."

- "You really wanted this project to make a difference."

- "You thought it was important enough to try."

- "Even though you didn't get the results you wanted, you stuck to your guns."

- "You knocked it out of the park!"

- "That really took courage on your part."

- "Your patience and determination to stick to the issue at hand were really effective in that discussion."

Reflections

Reflections involve listening carefully to what the other person is saying and then offering back some aspect of what was said in the form of a statement. Reflective listening is considered the cornerstone of MI, and is equally important in MI-Lead, as it is the single most important skill when it comes to fostering change in others. Why is this? The answer lies with the many important functions that reflections serve.

First, reflections demonstrate to the other individual that we are listening and paying close attention. This in and of itself is incredibly powerful. Human beings are social creatures and, as such, we crave feeling heard and understood by others. It is a basic human need.

Second, reflections are validating. When we offer back what the other has said, we are not offering any judgment about what was said; instead we are merely accepting what was said. Similarly, when we are reflecting, we are also avoiding the righting reflex that we discussed earlier. That is, we are not advising, recommending, educating, informing, or otherwise trying to fix. Likewise, reflections help to minimize discord (which we will discuss in more detail in a later chapter), as they avoid argument and disagreement.

Third, reflections encourage elaboration and invite the other individual to contribute to the direction of the conversation. This includes giving the individual the opportunity to respond to our reflections by further elaborating or clarifying, which helps us as well as the other individual better understand what was meant by his or her original statement.

Finally, reflections evoke, reinforce, and generate more change talk than even questions do. By selectively choosing what to reflect, we are pulling for change talk, providing additional opportunities for the individual to hear their own change talk, and encouraging the individual to continue to discuss change (that is, engaging in additional change talk). And since change talk predicts change, it becomes apparent why reflections are so central to facilitating the change process. Well-placed reflections can move mountains.

Perhaps you are wondering exactly how to reflect successfully. Reflections are statements that involve offering some element of what was said back to the speaker and giving him or her the opportunity to respond (for example, by clarifying, elaborating, agreeing, etc.). Reflections might be formed from something a person explicitly stated, implied, or indicated with emotions or body language. Reflections are not questions; your voice will go down at the end of the statement, not up. Consider the following responses after an individual tells you they didn't complete something in time.

- "You missed the deadline?" [your tone raises at the end]

- "You missed the deadline." [your tone drops or stays the same at the end]

If you have any doubt about the difference in the potential impact of these two statements on the individual or in the potential responses you may receive from using them, try saying them out loud. Better yet, try using them on a colleague, using the two different approaches and ask for feedback on how each felt. You will likely find that the first response felt like a judgment and led to defensiveness, while the second response felt validating (or sounded more matter-of-fact) and led to elaboration. Reflections that end with the tone of voice rising can come across as closed-ended questions or, worse, as judgments. We recommend, instead, that you lower your tone at the end of the reflection. As simple as this sounds, you may find that it requires practice and diligence.

It is worth noting here that, generally speaking, there are two types of reflections: simple and complex. Both have their time and place, and they can have a remarkably different impact. *Simple reflections* stick to the content of what the speaker said and do not go below the surface. They can be a repetition or a rephrase, but they do not offer anything beyond what was said. Here are some examples of each in response to the following statement: "I don't have time to take on another project."

- "You don't have time to take on another project." (repetition)

- "You don't have time to take on something new." (rephrase)

In both cases the response stuck to the content that was offered. In the first case, the statement was simply repeated. In the second, the statement was rephrased from "another project" to "something new." Both are highly likely to be accurate and demonstrate to the speaker that the responder was listening. Each may even elicit some elaboration on the part of the speaker. An equally likely response to such a reflection is for the speaker to agree and offer little to no elaboration. Thus, the downside to simple reflections is that, because they fail to offer anything new, they can quickly evoke annoyance from the speaker if used too frequently ("Uh, yeah, that's what I said."). Thus, we recommend using these sparingly, and typically more so at the beginning of a conversation (when little beyond the surface content of what is being said is known or suspected) or when you are stumped as to what is being said or how to respond. Once you have more information to work with, we recommend complex reflections.

Complex reflections go below the surface. They reflect emotions behind the speaker's statement, take a guess at underlying meaning, or even attempt to continue the paragraph (that is, anticipate where the speaker is going with the next statement). Complex reflections are much more likely to elicit elaboration and keep the conversation going relative to simple reflections, although it should be noted that an accurate complex reflection can still elicit simple agreement without any elaboration ("Yeah, exactly!"). Complex reflections are also more engaging because they require more attention (to both verbal and non-verbal language) and greater effort to understand from the listener. They also encourage the speaker to understand and talk about themselves at a deeper level.

Complex reflections also tend to guide more than simple reflections. That is, they allow the listener to be more active in contributing to the direction of the conversation. A simple reflection sticks to the speaker's content; thus, no additional meaning or direction is offered. A complex reflection goes beyond what was said and can focus on any element of what was implied, meant but not said, or emoted. This gives the listener much more latitude and offers an opportunity to guide the conversation toward a mutually defined goal. Consider where the conversation might go based on the following complex reflections to the following statement: "I don't have time to take on another project."

- "You need more time." (reflecting underlying meaning)

- "You're frustrated that you don't have time to work on this new project." (reflecting emotion)

- "If you had more time, you'd be interested in taking on this new project." (continuing the paragraph)

In each case above, the speaker's response to the reflection will likely be to elaborate on the reflection, and thus to further discuss how or why to find more time to work on existing or new projects. Notice how this differs from the likely response to the simple reflections noted above, which will undoubtedly center around lack of time or inability to take on something else. In other words, the simple reflections above will more likely than not elicit sustain talk, primarily because we reflected sustain talk (and nothing else). When we reflect on the person's reasons or need to change, as in the examples immediately above, we are much more likely to elicit change talk. Complex reflections give us much more opportunity to reflect change, as they allow us to go beyond the confines of what was explicitly stated.

Before we move on to the last of our OARS, let's take a look at and discuss a few more reflections. Consider the following responses to an individual, we'll call David, who states, "It's really hard for me to arrive on time. I'm not a morning person, and it's hard getting the kids ready for school, especially being a single parent. I know I need to get this figured out, but I really can't seem to make it work."

How might each of the reflections below guide where the conversation goes next?

- "You can't make it work." (simple reflection)

- "It sounds like mornings are difficult for you." (simple reflection)

- "It sounds like you're really concerned about this." (reflecting emotion)

- "You're wondering how you might be able to overcome these hurdles." (reflecting underlying meaning)

What do you make of that last reflection? Some individuals, especially those new to reflecting, are concerned about taking a guess at what the speaker truly means by a statement. In the above example, David never directly says anything about considering strategies to overcome morning obstacles. Wouldn't it be presumptuous to put these words in his mouth? What if I guess wrong?

First of all, we have some evidence in David's words that the above reflection might actually be accurate. After all, he does acknowledge that he needs to make changes, and his final statement implies that he has tried some strategies. So it's not too far-fetched to think that he's currently thinking of other strategies.

Second, and this is the more important point, if we are truly listening and seeking to understand an individual, *we are rarely punished for guessing wrong.* Instead, the speaker is likely to elaborate if we're right, and correct us if we're wrong. Either way, we get additional information. If we are truly engaged with the individual, inaccurate reflections are not likely to be met with scorn, disbelief, or contempt, especially if the reflection is plausible based on some element of what was said (currently or previously) or how it was stated. Generally speaking, complex reflections guide the conversation more quickly and effectively towards change, so we recommend using them more frequently than simple reflections, and making guesses through reflecting when it comes to understanding the other individual.

Summaries

Summaries are a series of reflections that bring in multiple elements of what the speaker has said. They have multiple uses in motivational interviewing. During the engaging process, summaries can demonstrate to the speaker that we've been paying close attention. For example, "You mentioned that you're having difficulty arriving on time consistently. You're not a morning person, you have to get the kids ready for school, and nothing you've tried seems to work."

During any of the four processes, summaries can also be used to elicit additional elaboration. For example, "It sounds like you want to make sure you get to work on time because you want to keep your job, be more productive, and demonstrate that you're a team player. What else?" An open-ended, evocative question following the summary, as in the preceding example, can help with eliciting more information, although it is often not necessary. The summary itself invites additional elaboration.

Summaries can also be used in the focusing process to help transition from one topic to another. In this case, a summary can nicely wrap-up the discussion of one topic, especially by highlighting change talk (including any commitment language that you heard), and pave the way for discussing a new topic. For example, "It sounds like you have several reasons for wanting to get to work on time more consistently. You've been thinking about several different ways you might accomplish this, and you'd like to start this week by making and implementing a morning schedule with your kids. Sounds like a solid plan. What would you think about spending some time discussing last week's project."

Finally, summaries can be used to transition from the evoking process to planning, or at least see if the speaker is ready to do so. Evocative, open-ended questions immediately following the summary can be especially useful here. For example, "It sounds like you have several reasons for wanting to get to work on time more consistently. You've had some ideas about how you might accomplish this, and you're thinking it might start with a discussion with your kids. So what's next?" If David, the speaker, is ready to make a plan, his likely response is to start describing some initial or next steps that he is ready and/or willing to take. If so, you are in the planning process. If he is not ready for planning, his likely response to the summary and evocative question will be some type of sustain talk. This is also useful information, as it indicates that there is still some work to be done in the evoking process. Either way, the evocative, open-ended question is very useful following the summary, and can help you test the water to see if David is ready for planning. Some example open-ended questions for accomplishing this are presented below:

- "What do you make of this?"

- "Where does this leave you?"

- "So where do you go from here?"

- "What's the first (next) step?"

One final thought before we leave summaries. As with individual reflections, you choose what to reflect in your summary. Your choice for what to reflect depends on what you hope to accomplish. If your primary goal is to engage with the speaker, then reflecting any of his main points, whether sustain talk, change talk, or unrelated speech, can be useful. However, if you're in the evoking process, especially if you're attempting to transition into planning, it's more useful to stay away from reflecting sustain talk while offering a summary, and to primarily include reflections of change talk. In your summary, reflecting less of the individual's or team's sustain talk and more of the change talk tends to elicit additional talk about change, and the more change talk there is, the more likely the individual or team is to ultimately engage in the targeted change.

It should be worth noting here that tone of voice is an important component for all of the OARS. We already mentioned one role of tone of voice when it comes to reflections, but, more generally, we think it's important to state explicitly that tone is important no matter which MI-Lead skill you are implementing. If any of the OARS are spoken in an irritated, challenging, judgmental, or sarcastic tone, this is likely to elicit sustain talk or possibly even lead to discord. Instead, a warm, compassionate, and curious tone is more likely to engage the other individual and elicit change talk. In short, keep the MI spirit in mind and use it as a guiding force in terms of both what you say and how you say it.

So, how do the OARS support effective leadership? Let's look at an example. A supervisor over a customer service department, we'll call her Maria, was having difficulties convincing staff to follow through with what she saw as a simple process of faxing, scanning, and filing customer paperwork. Looking for help, she sought out an MI-Lead consultant and stressed that "I don't understand what in the world is wrong with this employee?" She shared that she had held a few meetings during which she told staff what to do and how she wanted it done. She was frustrated and couldn't understand why her staff weren't just following through with her directives.

The consultant inquired more about her discussions with the staff, specifically about what types of questions she may have asked to see what the employees' thoughts were or to hear what their plan might be. Maria reflected that she hadn't considered the employees' perspectives, instead assuming that her staff saw value in her directives in the same way that she did. After a bit of discussion about this realization and about how she might apply the MI-Lead tools in this scenario, she decided to approach the next staff meeting with curiosity; she determined that she would try "asking" more and "telling" less with the goal of listening, understanding, and empowering. After the meeting, she reported being impressed with the staff response, but, even more importantly, she noted that, over the course of the next few weeks, staff had appeared more motivated, making positive changes in their system for managing customer paperwork and resolving many of the issues independently and without her direction.

Let's talk about how Maria accomplished her goal. She went in knowing the long-term goal she wanted to impact. After talking to the staff about the long term goal, she used *open-ended questions* to learn about their thoughts, what they saw as the barriers for success, and what they believed could be done to most effectively impact that goal. She responded with *affirmations* for their efforts, their commitment, and their ideas which helped the staff feel more confident and acknowledged. These open questions and affirmations empowered them and helped them to feel a sense of ownership for improving the system. She demonstrated that she was really listening to the staff with the goal of understanding their perspective by using *reflections* which helped staff feel heard and deepened the discussion. *Summaries* were used to help transition their discussion into an examination of specific, next steps.

Let's take a look at a dialogue that uses these steps in a leadership situation:

Team Member: "I'm just not sure adding another program right now is a good thing."

Leader: "Tell me what you think might be a good strategy to use right now." (Open-ended question)

T: "With a small team and all the pressure we have on us right now, I think the focus should be on getting more members."

L: "You see the top priority as needing to get more team members, and once we resolve this issue everything will be ok." (reflection)

T: "Yes, I really think that's what we need to focus on. Everything else can wait until then."

L: "You've put a lot of thought into this, and you're quite invested in making sure our team does well." (affirmation)

T: "Yeah. I've been here a long time and I enjoy what we do."

L: "I'm pleased to hear that! May I share some information with you? (Team Member nods) We are working very hard to obtain new members, and I would be very happy to share with you our progress as we work to get more."

T: "Oh, I didn't realize. I mean, I figured, but didn't know. I'm really glad to hear that, and I would appreciate updates."

L: "Great, I'll make sure I keep you updated. While we work through those issues, what else do you think we could do, that could make a strong impact?" (Open-ended question)

T: "Well...I know there are some systems that are broken, and we've really needed to do some system redesign projects on them, but we really haven't had the time to do so."

L: "Not only you, but the whole team feels there are some broken systems causing more workload. You know what they are and just need the resources and time to implement a proper plan for a system redesign." (Reflection)

When you read this example, you can begin to see how the MI-Lead is being integrated into the conversation. The conversation is a coaching one to support team members as they create their own path. Let's complete the following exercises to practice using OARS.

Exercise 6.1

Turn the following closed-ended questions into open-ended questions. Some suggestions for each question are offered below.

1. Did you look at the numbers?

2. Have you completed your project?

3. Will you go through all the data?

4. Do you have thoughts about the trainings?

5. Are you finding all this information about decreasing production time useful?

6. Are you meeting the customer's needs?

7. Will you start collecting the completed surveys and collate the data?

8. Have you completed the tasks I asked you to do on the new computer system?

_____

_____

Now let's look at some possible open-ended questions for each of the above examples:

1. What are your thoughts about the numbers? How's the data review going?

2. Where are you with your project? How's the project coming along?

3. What do you plan to do with the data? Tell me what you make of the data.

4. What do you think about the trainings? How can we maximize the impact of the trainings?

5. What do you make of this new information? What ideas does your team have for decreasing production time from start to finish?

6. How are you doing at meeting the customer's needs? When it comes to meeting your customers' needs, tell me about your strengths and where could you see getting even better yet?

7. Where are you with regard to collecting the completed surveys and collating the data? How's it going with data collection and collation?

8. How are you doing with the trainings on the new computer system? What's your feedback on the computer system trainings?

Exercise 6.2

Write a simple and complex reflection for each statement below.

1. I've definitely burnt the candle at both ends to get this project up and running. I hope it's what you're looking for.

Simple reflection:

_____
_____
_____

Complex reflection:

_____
_____
_____

2. To tell you the truth, I really don't have a clue on why customer service is so low. The customers seem to think everything is bad.

Simple reflection:

_____
_____
_____

Complex reflection:

_____
_____
_____

3. When I took on this project I didn't realize there would be so many angry people that I would have to deal with.

Simple reflection:

_____
_____
_____

Complex reflection:

_____
_____
_____

4. We just need more staff. All of our problems revolve around that one issue. Staffing!

Simple reflection:

_____
_____
_____

Complex reflection:

_____
_____
_____

5. This data set is overwhelming. I'm not even sure where to start or what to do with it.

Simple reflection:

_____
_____
_____

Complex reflection:

_____
_____
_____

6. I think we have some great ideas that have been presented. It's just a matter of identifying which one and when to start.

Simple reflection:

_____
_____
_____

Complex reflection:

_____
_____
_____

7. Ever since you've arrived, we've had issues and morale has gone down. The system is a mess, and it's making it so we can't get things done.

Simple reflection:

_____
_____
_____

Complex reflection:

_____
_____
_____

Below are some examples of simple and complex reflections in response to each of the statements above.

1. "I've definitely burnt the candle at both ends to get this project up and running. I hope it's what you're looking for."

Simple reflection: *"You've been working hard on this project."*

Complex reflection: *"You're really hoping all your hard work pays off.*

2. "To tell you the truth, I really don't have a clue on why customer service is so low. The customers seem to think everything is bad."

Simple reflection: *You're not sure why customer service is rated so low.*

Complex reflection: *"You're concerned about our customer service ratings and think we should do something about them."*

3. "When I took on this project I didn't realize there would be so many angry people that I would have to deal with."

Simple reflection: *"You didn't know you were going to be dealing with so many angry individuals."*

Complex reflection: *"This project has presented you with some challenges that you weren't expecting."*

4. "We just need more staff. All of our problems revolve around that one issue. Staffing!"

Simple reflection: *"Staffing is our main problem."*

Complex reflection: *"You feel it's such a simple issue, and you're frustrated that we haven't done more to address it."*

5. "This data set is overwhelming. I'm not even sure where to start or what to do with it."

Simple reflection: *"You're not sure where to go from here."*

Complex reflection: *"You're looking for some guidance."*

6. I think we have some great ideas that have been presented. It's just a matter of identifying which one and when to start.

Simple reflection: *You think some of the ideas you heard are really good.*

Complex reflection: *You're excited about getting started and have some ideas about how and when.*

7. Ever since you've arrived, we've had issues and morale has gone down. The system is a mess, and it's making it so we can't get things done.

Simple reflection: *You think the system is broken.*

Complex reflection: *You feel that I'm the reason morale has gone down and that I haven't done enough to address the system's issues.*

Chapter 7

Working through Ambivalence

When an individual or team is considering engaging in a particular behavior or change and is *ambivalent*, they feel two ways about the behavior. Ambivalence is a normal part of the change process, and demonstrating an appreciation for and understanding of an individual or team's ambivalence can help to resolve the ambivalence. You as a leader can help those you lead resolve their ambivalence by emphasizing your respect for their autonomy, encouraging collaboration, and evoking their own reasons for making an individual or an organizational change. Let's spend some time discussing how to do this.

Resolving Ambivalence

As a leader, you likely have ideas about what needs to be done, why it should be done, and how it should be done, but what do you do if those you lead don't share your "what", "why", or "how?" These challenges can feel frustrating, especially if you feel there is nothing you can do to motivate your group, and, depending on how you respond, you can either widen the ambivalence gap or decrease it. You might be tempted to take a commanding stance, taking on the Theory X management style mentioned in Chapter One, a style in which you demand the required behavior and outline the punitive consequences of failing to engage in it. If the consequences are negative enough, the individual or team may even engage in the desired behavior or needed change while the consequences are in place…but at what cost?

A great deal of research has been dedicated to assessing the effect of punishment on behavior. While *reinforcers* increase the likelihood that a behavior will occur, *punishers* decrease the likelihood that a behavior will occur. Punishers actually serve to suppress the undesirable behavior rather than increasing the likelihood that an alternative, more desirable behavior will occur. While the threat of punishment may remove an undesired behavior in the short term, there are some drawbacks:

- Punishment only suppresses the undesirable behavior; thus if you remove the punishment, the undesirable behavior returns.

- Punishment increases resentment and decreases collaboration, leading to lower motivation in the future.

- Punishment can cause fear and mistrust that interferes with creativity and independent thinking.

- Punishment informs an individual about what not to do, rather than what *to* do.

If the longer term goal is to increase an individual or team's collaboration, their motivation for change, and their sense of personal responsibility for the change while maintaining creativity and satisfaction, reinforcement is a more effective way to facilitate change. This approach of finding out what is meaningful to the employee in order to facilitate motivation is more consistent with Chapter One's Theory Y and transformational leadership management styles and tends to foster a collaborative approach to problem solving while minimizing resentment and mistrust.

Finding Common Ground

Determining an individual's reasons and/or motivations for change is not as simple as identifying our own reasons for engaging in the behavior and assuming that the individual's reasons are the same. What motivates you for change may not be what motivates others for change, and what motivates one team member for change is not necessarily the same as what motivates another team member to engage in the same behavior. Additionally, what motivates a team may not be what motivates the organization that oversees the team or group. The challenge is in finding each individual's reasons for engaging in the target behavior, reasons that are valuable (or reinforcing) to the individual or team, to you the leader, and to the organization itself. Without an understanding of the individual's (and the organization's) ideas about what is important, about their own reasons for valuing a behavior or change, and about their ideas for how best to achieve a goal, it is unlikely that you as a leader will be able to effectively facilitate that individual's or team's motivation to engage in a target behavior. That understanding comes only through discussion, curiosity, open questions, and active listening: the approaches and techniques of MI-Lead.

Let's consider an example. If a clothing chain called Ana Tyler requests that all of its employees working on the floor wear clothing representative of that retail chain, it may be because the Ana Tyler clothing company would like for their employees to provide additional advertising for the company's clothing while working, leading to increased sales and greater corporate profits. Trish, a supervisor of the employees at one of the stores, may encourage her employees to wear Ana Tyler's clothing in order to increase sales at her store and thus ensure that she receives a bonus at the end of the year. Lacy, a floor employee, may wish to wear Ana Tyler's styles because she receives a 15% discount on anything she purchases from the store. Another employee may choose to wear the store's clothing styles because fashions from Ana Tyler fit her better than any other similar stores. Finally, another employee may value her sense of independence and her freedom of self-expression, and she may be reluctant to purchase and wear traditional styles from Ana Tyler if she feels she is being coerced. It may be important to her to feel that she has picked out her own styles that support her freedom of self-expression.

As a leader, your approach to motivating these individuals with MI-Lead ideally would be to look at their unique aspects of "what," "why", and "how" to change. Through asking and listening, you will be able to engage the person, find common ground, and elicit the individual's own thoughts about what to change, reasons for change, and ideas for how to achieve that goal, and these ideas are likely to benefit not only those you lead in terms of motivation and satisfaction but also you as the leader and the organization itself. Herein lies the value in seeking out common ground with those you lead.

Eliciting Change Talk (As discussed in Chapter 5)

When someone is ambivalent about engaging in a particular change, the individual can generally provide you with arguments for both engaging in the change and reasons for not engaging in the change. Arguments for engaging in the change include statements about the positive consequences of engaging in the desired change and the downside of not engaging in the change. This is called *change talk* and includes statements of *desire* to engage in the change, of *ability* to be successful in engaging in the change, of *reasons* for engaging in the change, of *need* for the change, of *commitment* to engaging in the change, of a consideration of imminent action (*activating* language), and/or of a review of recent steps taken (*taking steps*) around the change.

Statements arguing against engaging in the desired change are called *sustain talk* and include reviewing the negative consequences of engaging in the change and benefits of maintaining the status quo or current way of doing things. The literature shows us that when change talk is elicited from the individual who is considering change, the likelihood of engaging in the change process increases.

However, when sustain talk is elicited from the individual who is considering a new change, the likelihood of change decreases. Finally, when we as leaders are the ones making the argument for an individual to engage in a particular change, the ambivalent individual is likely to respond with sustain talk. It's human nature. Unfortunately, when our approach encourages the other individual to argue and/or respond with sustain talk, the outcome is not neutral. By eliciting sustain talk from the individual, we as leaders have made the targeted change <u>less</u> likely to occur. In our attempts to help, we've actually made things worse!

Avoiding the Righting Reflex (As discussed in Chapter 4)

You as a leader may be confident in your reasons for requesting particular changes or behaviors. You may see the behavior or change as a logical solution to an identified problem, and, at times, you may seek to convince those you lead of your ideas and reasons behind them without taking the time to ask and listen to their thoughts. Generally, our attempts to offer our own solutions to others for why and how to solve a problem come from a genuine desire to "fix" the problem. You may recall from Chapter Four that this attempt to "fix" the problem is called the *Righting Reflex.* However, by deciding what the solution should be, why it should be, and how it should look without considering the thoughts and ideas of the individual or team, you are likely to generate pushback while reducing the likelihood of change. By providing your own ideas for solutions, you have threatened the individual's sense of autonomy.

At her MI trainings, Dr. Theresa Moyers has shared a funny example that demonstrates the fact that human nature is to argue the other side. Imagine for a moment that you have a close female friend who comes to you to talk about her frustration in a romantic relationship:

"My boyfriend is driving me crazy. He's been living with me for a year now, saying he's looking for a job, but all he really does is sit around all day in his boxers playing video games. I come home exhausted after work to find the apartment a mess, no groceries in

the house, and there he sits, doing absolutely nothing! ..and do you know what he had the gall to say to me last night when I got home late?"

" 'What's for dinner'!"

Now, imagine that you, being the good friend that you are, respond to her complaints with:

"You should just get rid of him. He's dead weight. You can do so much better!"

Keeping in mind human nature, how do you imagine that your female friend is likely to respond? Most of us will guess some version of the following:

" ..but I love him..I can't imagine my life without him.."

Now, imagining the same scenario (your friend complains and you prepare to respond), but this time you respond with:

"Maybe you should cut him a little slack. I think he really cares ... after all, remember that time you were sick with a stomach bug and he tried to make you homemade chicken soup? I think his heart is in the right place."

How do you imagine that your friend will respond this time? Considering human nature, perhaps she will respond with clear frustration:

"You just don't get it! You're not the one who has to live with him! He's making me crazy!"

This dialogue is not neutral. In your genuine attempt to help, you are actually making your friend less likely to engage in your recommended solution (leaving her boyfriend or staying with him) by eliciting sustain talk from her. Your argument for engaging in a particular behavior actually encourages your friend to give you reasons for NOT engaging in that behavior. Research has shown us that the more sustain talk that comes out of an individual's mouth, the less likely it is that he or she will engage in that behavior or process change. Conversely, the more change talk verbalized by an individual, the more likely it is that he or she will eventually engage in the change. *No matter how wise or technically correct you may be, arguments for change that come from you do NOT predict eventual and sustained change in those you lead.* Your arguments for change actually predict that the ambivalent individual will argue in the opposite direction!

The key, therefore, to facilitating an individual's motivation for a particular behavior or system change is to find out about his or her own ideas about reaching a particular goal and why and how the individual believes that those changes should occur. There are several tools for evoking and responding to this change talk from those you lead.

Eliciting and Responding to Change Talk

The components of OARS introduced in previous chapters are essential to evoking change talk and resolving ambivalence about engaging in a specific, individual or organizational change. Open-ended questions can include hypothetical scenarios, looking forward, encouraging elaboration, the ruler exercises, identification of goals and values, and coming alongside. Each of these are explained and demonstrated below.

When a person does not view a particular goal or change as important, *hypothetical questions* can encourage them to begin considering what change might look like but without the pressure of having to commit to it. For example, you might ask someone who is only putting in the minimum amount of work, time, and effort into a program,

"If you were going to make some changes to increase the quantity and quality of the programs you are developing, what do you imagine you might do?"

The person is likely to respond with change talk by identifying the how of a particular change. The individual will likely talk about what could be done (ability) and may even be considering taking steps towards that goal.

You may encourage another leader in your organization to *look forward* when considering ideas for change that will benefit the leader as well as the organization and those the individual leads,

"If you look ahead 6 months or even one year from now, how do you imagine outcomes will look if you engage in this change... and if you don't?"

The leader is likely to describe benefits of engaging in the change and consequences of failing to engage in the change, both of which are change talk, thus increasing the likelihood that the individual will eventually engaging in the change.

As you begin to hear change talk, you can facilitate additional change talk by reflecting what you hear and *encouraging elaboration*, for example,

"It sounds like this is something you've been giving some serious thought about."

And then, after he or she responds to your reflection,

"Tell me more about that."

Another strategy for eliciting change talk is using a *ruler exercise* to determine level of importance of or confidence in an individual's ability to successfully engage in a change. For example,

"On a scale of 1-10, with ten being the most important, how important is it to you to [targeted change]?"

If higher than a one, you might ask,

"A [chosen number], why that and not [a number slightly lower than the chosen number]?"

For example, *"A six. Why a six and not a three or four?"*

It is important to ask why the individual did not respond with a lower number as opposed to a higher one. The response to being asked why not a lower number is likely to be change talk, whereas asking why the number isn't higher is likely to yield sustain talk.

If the number is a one, you might ask the below question instead,

"What would it take to increase that number even just a little bit to a [slightly higher than the chosen number]?"

For example, *"What would it take to increase the one even just a little to, maybe, a two?"*

For example, *"What would it take to increase the six even just a little bit to a seven?"*

The response to this question might be additional change talk and/or provide you with some ideas about what could be in place to make it even more important (and therefore likely) for change to happen. This ruler and set of follow up questions can be slightly modified to assess and enhance confidence by substituting "confident" for "important" in the above questions.

For example, *"On a scale of 1-10, how confident are you that you can adjust this process for completing customer paperwork?"*

One of the most effective ways to elicit change talk and ultimately increase motivation is to explore an individual's *goals, values,* or *priorities*, separate from the change being considered, and then encouraging that individual to tell you about how the behavior or system change being considered fits with these goals or values.

"Putting aside [the change being considered] for a moment, what are some goals or values that are important in your life? What do

you consider to be the most important value that you hold?" "And how does [the change being considered] fit in with that value?"

For example, *"You said that the most important thing in your life is to know that you are giving back to others...how would your working at the soup kitchen you mentioned fit in with that value of serving others?"*

Sometimes, despite your best efforts to elicit change talk related to engaging in a targeted behavior or process change, you may recognize that the individual is just not ready, willing, or interested in making a change. You may realize that, while you are using the above listed strategies in exploring the possibility of change, the individual is responding with predominantly sustain talk (talk that supports the status quo) rather than change talk. Remembering that increased sustain talk is associated with a decreased likelihood of change, you may decide to *come alongside*, which may effectively end the discussion around the currently considered target behavior and eliminate further sustain talk around it. Coming alongside involves acknowledging that the individual is not ready for change, despite their desire, ability, reasons, or need for change. This preserves trust and respect for autonomy that you have developed in your relationship with the individual and leaves the door open for change at a later time should circumstances change.

"It is clear that, at this point, you don't feel that you are able to volunteer on the PTA. Despite your belief that your ideas would be helpful in expanding the work that the PTA does, you don't feel able to fully commit to this additional activity right now."

Often, following a statement that indicates that you are coming alongside, you may want to add an additional open question, asking the individual what it might take for him or her to decide that he or she is ready for change at a later time.

"What would need to happen for you to decide that the time has come to volunteer with the PTA and get your ideas out there? What would make the pros of joining outweigh the cons?"

This type of open question may actually elicit some last change talk while still supporting the individual's autonomy to decide if and when a change is the right choice.

At any time that you are utilizing the above listed strategies, you can gauge how well the conversation is going, remembering that more change talk from an individual specific to an identified behavior or process is predictive of that individual's following through with change and remembering that increased sustain talk predicts that the individual will be less likely to engage in that change. You can listen to those you lead and determine how helpful the discussion is by paying attention to whether you are eliciting change talk or sustain talk. If there is an increase in sustain talk, you may decide to adjust your sails a bit and try a different approach that demonstrates empathy and a desire to better understand what is important to that team member.

Let's look at the following scenario in which a leader attempts to address ambivalence with two employees. If the leader considers what is important to each employee, he may find that, in doing so, each employee has very different ideas about the targeted change; their sources of motivation may be quite different. As a result, the approach to working with the employees may differ as well.

Jonathan is a regional supervisor for the Florida division of a national equipment company called MoveIT! He supervises 300 employees including the regional manager of sales (Andy) and the regional manager of rentals (Ron).

During a financial review meeting, Jonathan is informed that one of MoveIT!'s larger clients, a big box store, who is a source of large amounts of revenue through both the sales and the rental divisions of the company, has not paid it's rental accounts in nine months. When Ron has contacted the big box store accounting department about the outstanding balance, their reply has been that it was an oversight occurring as a result of a great deal of turnover in the past year. Despite assurances that the rental balance will be immediately paid in full, the pending payment does not arrive and the balance due grows to over $100,000. Jonathan brings this up at two consecutive monthly manager meetings, emphasizing to both Ron and Andy that maintaining a relationship with this company is a priority as is getting the delinquent rental account paid in full.

Andy notes that the sales accounts are current and that he continues to enjoy a very good relationship with the big box store managers, with sales higher this year than in the past 3 years combined. Jonathan stresses to both Ron and Andy that the problem needs to be resolved. At the quarterly managers' meeting the following month, Jonathan notes that the balance due on the rental account remains outstanding, that Ron has not had any success in getting the accounting department at the big box store to settle the debt, that he has instead placed a hold on the account which suspends all rental activity by this big box store until the payment is made in full, and that Andy has not assisted the Ron in getting the bill paid. When Jonathan points these facts out, the two regional managers begin to argue; Ron stating that he could have used some help in reaching someone in the company that would be willing to resolve the issue and Andy stating that his side of the MoveIT! business is thriving and that assisting the rental division in collecting its outstanding balances is not his job.

What complaints do you imagine Jonathan may have at this quarterly meeting?

What are Jonathan's goals? What is his agenda? What would he like from each of these employees? What is Andy's agenda? And what is Ron's agenda?

Jonathan is likely upset that the two managers are approaching the customer, the big box store, as separate silos that have little to no impact on one another rather than approaching the customer as a team. Perhaps Jonathan would like for both managers to look at what will benefit their own company as a whole rather than just concerning themselves with their portion of the company. Jonathan might suggest that his managers "should" be concerned about what's best for the entire company even if it leads to additional work or effort on their part. He might even demand that Andy assist Ron in clearing these debts before the following monthly meeting.

While the managers may follow through with his demands, what is the likelihood that they will continue to quibble over whose responsibility the work is and fail to take collective responsibility for the company's overall well-being?

How might Jonathan utilize the principles of MI-Lead to successfully address his concerns with his employees? Recalling that the following four processes are not necessarily linear and that it will be important for Jonathan to identify where each employee is in terms of process in order to adjust his own approach, consider the following:

Process 1: *Engage*

Speak with each employee about what he feels is important in this situation. Use open-ended questions, reflect, affirm successes and strengths, and summarize.

Process 2: *Focus / Find a shared agenda*

Provide feedback. Be curious. What is important to each employee? What is motivating the individual's behavior? What is the individual's agenda? The goal is to ask and accept. Find out what each employee's thoughts are about the feedback. What does each individual believe should be the target for change? What are the individual's ideas for addressing the problem? What is the worst-case scenario if no changes are made? What is the best-case scenario if changes are made? Use the importance ruler and/or the confidence ruler. Use OARS.

Process 3: *Elicit change talk and soften sustain talk*
Reflect change talk about the target behavior. Encourage elaboration. Use variations of open-ended questions such as looking forward. Stay solution focused versus problem focused. When sustain talk is present, refrain from reinforcing the sustain talk and instead use the OARS skills discussed earlier to elicit change talk.

Emphasize autonomy. When an individual is absolutely not ready for change as evidenced by a great deal of sustain talk without significant change talk, consider coming alongside in order to preserve the relationship and the potential for future examination of the possibility of change.

Process 4: *Encourage each team member to make a plan*

Affirm. Consider potential barriers and problem solve around those barriers. Identify factors that will help the individual succeed with the plan. Remember that it isn't change talk if the ideas come out of the leader's mouth. Arrange follow-up to review each individual's efforts. Follow through with the follow-up!

Let's consider each process during a hypothetical discussion between Jonathan (J) and Ron (R). Notice that Jonathan starts the conversation with engaging.

J: Good morning Ron. I know this has been a busy week and appreciate your coming by. I know that you've expressed some frustration with collection efforts for BigBox.com (*Engaging* by affirming Ron's busy schedule and his willingness to meet with him), and I'm hoping we can examine this (*Focusing*).

R: Thanks. I've been really frustrated with these folks. We have sent them monthly bills regularly and to no avail. We've gotten no response.

J: You've worked really hard to manage this challenge within your department, and you're frustrated that you haven't seen results (Reflecting as part of *Focusing*; continues to build trust).

R: Yes. It's really important to me that my guys see me as competent in spite of being relatively new to this position, and I hate having to rely on Andy's (Sales Manager's) relationships and networks within the company to get things done. At the same time, it seems like Andy could have helped put me in touch with the right people in the company to help get this resolved. Now it seems like I'm going to have a tense relationship with the rental folks at Big-

Box.com, which isn't going to help us meet our target numbers this quarter.

J: You value your position and you would like to earn the respect of your team, and you would also like to know that others have your back too. You want to maintain a good relationship with the companies we have contracts with, and you want to see the outstanding balances paid on time (More *reflecting* of what's important to Ron, what his goals are, and what challenges he is encountering; explore further using a reflection to encourage elaboration; *Evoking* more change talk).

R: Yes. Exactly. I want my team to know that I won't quit on them. That I will keep working hard just like they do until the job is done. I wouldn't have minded if Andy had reached out to help put me in touch with the right people in the company though. I feel like I'm set up to fail here, either I piss off the Big-Box folks in order to get their account paid up or I have this outstanding balance that I can't show as paid in full.

J: You don't like either option and would like to find a better one (*Evoking* more change talk with a double-sided reflection that first reflects the sustain talk and then reflects the change talk). Looking forward, say, by next quarter, how would you like to see things change? (Encourage additional change talk using an open question that asks Ron to look forward)

R: I'd like to get this account paid up, but I don't want to lose their business.

J: It also sounds like you'd like to develop a better relationship with Andy (solution focused versus problem focused during *evoking*).

J: Sounds like it might be helpful if we brainstorm some ways to get this resolved in a way that maintains your team's trust, encourages collaboration with our sales team, gets the charges paid in full, and supports future business with Big-Box.com.

R: Yes. I'd love to find a solution that does all that.

J: You'd like to identify a plan that will address all of these concerns. Where would you like to start? (Evoking begins to shift towards *Planning*; a reflection followed by an open question gives Ron an opportunity to identify his own ideas)

R: Well, I have an idea for how I might talk to folks at the Big-Box.com rental department to get their account paid up but that will also let them know that I am willing to work with them and that we want to keep their business.

J: Sounds like a great place to start. Tell me about your idea (*Planning*).

While progressing from Engaging to Planning is not always a linear process, it is helpful to remain aware of where your team member is in terms of the four processes, adjusting your approach to match your team member's readiness for change. How will you know if you push too quickly for a plan? You will begin to hear an increase in sustain talk or arguments against change and a decrease in change talk or discussion supporting change.

Chapter Summary

In summary, ambivalence about changing a particular behavior or about changing a process for doing things is normal. Motivation for engaging in a change requires that the change is important to the individual and that the individual is confident that he or she can successfully achieve his or her goal. Importance and confidence can only come from the individual who will engage in the change. As an individual engages in change talk, for example, talk about desire, ability, reasons, need, or actual plans for change, the likelihood that he or she will engage in that change increases. As an individual voices sustain talk, statements about desire, ability, reasons, need, or plans not to engage in a particular behavior, the likelihood that he or she will engage in the change process decreases. As a leader, you can facilitate resolution of ambivalence by supporting an individual's autonomy, seeking to understand his or her own motivations for change, and eliciting talk about that change. You may choose to focus on eliciting change talk by increasingly reflecting the change talk you hear and by asking for elaboration. You may find it helpful to avoid pushing your own agenda for change, instead working collaboratively towards an agenda that both you and those you lead share. This will increase an individual's satisfaction, ownership for choices, and motivation to follow through with the change process.

Chapter 8

Dancing with Discord

In the previous chapter, we discussed the nature of individual or team ambivalence. S*ustain talk* is likely to occur when an individual is ambivalent about change, and we indicated a few strategies for resolving ambivalence in the direction of change. But what if the situation is more challenging than ambivalence? What if the individual you're leading is disengaged, argumentative, stubborn, or otherwise reluctant to engage in behavior appropriate for the current organizational situation? In this chapter, we describe the distinction between sustain talk and the types of individual reactions noted above, which we collectively refer to as *discord*. We illustrate typical leadership responses to sustain talk and discord and how these responses tend to deteriorate the leader-led relationship and make lasting change less likely. We propose MI-consistent alternative responses that seek to both preserve (or enhance) the leader-led relationship and increase the likelihood that the individual will engage in the change process. Finally, we include examples of MI-consistent leadership responses to several common instances of difficult leader-led encounters.

For many years MI trainers, researchers, and clinicians discussed ways to address *resistance*, which was seen as any behavior from the other individual that indicated movement away from change. Resistance was a common term in MI trainings and papers, and these trainings and writings typically explained how to *roll with resistance*. This came to an end once the 3rd edition of MI was released in 2013, and with good reason. Resistance is a term that seems to treat a normal part of the change process (that is, not wanting to change) as abnormal or pathological. Resistance also puts the blame or responsibility for moving away from change squarely upon the shoulders of the other individual. It's as if we're describing a characteristic or shortcoming of the other person ("He's being resistant") without recognizing how we, as leaders, may be contributing to the issue. The trend within the training, practice, and research of MI has shifted in recent years away from the use of the term *resistance* and has moved instead toward the recognition of the phenomena of *sustain talk* and *discord* when describing movement away from change. Sustain talk, as noted previously, is any talk that favors staying the same. It is a normal part of the change process and is typically present when someone is ambivalent about change. Discord, on the other hand, represents a deterioration in the relationship between the leader and those being led.

Recognizing the difference between sustain talk and discord is useful in terms of knowing how to respond. With sustain talk, the goal is to minimize talk about staying the same, attempt to elicit and strengthen change talk, and to recognize when an individual may not be at all ready to change the behavior currently being discussed and to, therefore, move on. With discord, the goal is to (re)establish a positive relationship with the other individual, which may mean we need to return to the initial MI process of *engaging*. We've already discussed how and why sustain talk arises as well as some effective and ineffective responses to it. Before we discuss additional effective responses to both sustain talk and discord, let's take a closer look at discord.

Miller and Rollnick describe discord as "signals of disharmony in your collaborative relationship" (2013). They point to behaviors such as defending, squaring off, interrupting, and disengaging as examples of discord. Other behaviors may include arguing, "being stubborn", or attacking. These are valuable red flags that can help you become more aware of discord and then do something effective about it.

Leaders confronted with the above behaviors often become frustrated, disheartened, defensive, blaming, argumentative, etc. Some see this as an issue strictly with those they lead and think individuals engaging in these behaviors simply need to be removed from their role, position, or the organization. Even though there are appropriate times to remove an individual, it's important to remember there are also ways to work through many issues rather than simply getting rid of the person involved. When a leader does get argumentative or defensive, it often will only cause the situation to get worse. Rarely do those types of behaviors and actions help fix the problem.

Brian Kersh recalls being on the supervisee side of discord during a job he held several years ago:

I was given a major project with a hard deadline and was making significant progress on it initially. I was meeting regularly with my manager about the project, and he helped me develop short-term plans and goals as well as problem-solve around barriers that I was experiencing. This worked well for the first month or so of the project, until my manager left for an extended period of absence, leaving the assistant manager in charge. The assistant manager seemed less interested in my project, did not provide the same level of support, and assigned me many other tasks. What I assumed from the assistant manager's behavior was that the project was not that high of a priority, and as a result I spent less time working on it and did not make much progress under her supervision. Shortly before the manager's return, the assistant manager met with me to discuss my progress on the project. When she learned how little I had done, she became very upset, listed several mistakes I had made, blamed me for the lack of progress, discussed all the potential consequences of my lack of progress, including what would happen if I did not make an incredible amount of progress before the manager returned, and told me everything I needed to do over the coming weeks to improve the situation.

During this conversation with the assistant manager, I initially tried to defend my behaviors, but as the conversation continued, I outwardly shut down. I quit responding to her verbally, and my eyes adopted the "middle distant stare." Inwardly, I began thinking about what a bad supervisor she was, about how my lack of progress was really her fault, about how she was being totally irrational, and about how her behavior was likely being driven by her fear about how bad she was going to look once the manager returned and saw how little progress was made while he was out. Following this conversation, I did what I could to avoid the assistant manager and did little work on the project until the manager returned. What little work I did on the project during that time, I did with resentment and no internal motivation. Her conversation with me did little to change my behavior and left me with very little interest in working on a project that I had initially accepted so eagerly.

Shortly after his return, I met with the manager to discuss the project as well as my recent discussion with the assistant manager (she had clearly updated him on this prior to my meeting with him). In a calm, warm, and non-judgmental manner, he asked for my opinion on the factors that contributed to the limited progress on the project as well as on the unpleasant and non-productive meeting that the assistant manager and I recently had. As a result of this discussion, I became aware of and discussed how both the assistant manager and I had contributed to each of these issues. The manager also elicited from me ideas I had about getting back on track with the project as well as improving the working relationship between me and the assistant manager (I had no doubts that he had a similar conversation with her). Following this meeting, I re-doubled my efforts on the project and not only met the deadline but also later received an internal award for the quality of the work. In addition, the assistant manager and I both worked on improving communication with one another, and we successfully collaborated on subsequent projects.

This experience with discord became even more salient to me many years later as I came to better understand MI principles and strategies. When approached by the manager and assistant manager about my behaviors, both of whom had the same goals in their conversations with me, my response to their two styles was night and day. When approached with blame, labeling, and advice, I became defensive, shut down, and lost motivation for working on the project. When approached within a spirit of collaboration, evocation, and non-judgment, I became engaged, problem-solved, and recaptured motivation. Here I was, the same person in each discussion about my involvement on the project, and my behavior was strikingly different depending on the way I was approached.

This example illustrates an important point. When faced with a team member's ineffective or counter-productive behaviors, we are tempted to point out these behaviors, label or blame the person ("lazy," "oppositional," "poor time management skills," "poor team player"), highlight the negative impact of the chosen behavior, advise him or her on how to improve, or just "give 'em hell." In short, we engage in the righting reflex. It is important to note that these types of leadership behaviors, which are delivered with the intention of helping direct someone we lead in a productive manner, can, and often do, lead to discord.

But whether we as the leaders contribute to the discord or it simply "meets us at the door" (that is, it emerges as soon as we enter into the interaction with the other individual, without our contributing in any way other than simply being present), we are part of the disharmony, and we have a role to play in terms of bringing the relationship into harmony.

So, if the righting reflex (for example, giving the person knowledge, understanding, skills, or hell) is not the answer, what is? It may help at this point to re-examine the four processes of MI, and how discord can develop during any of them.

Discord can emerge during the *Engaging* process. As noted above, it can "meet us at the door," when we've seemingly done nothing to elicit it. For example, if you say to your team member, "Happy Friday, Joe!" and his response is "What's so happy about it? I guess *you* won't be working your butt off over the weekend trying to meet this deadline." If anything, you were trying to engage with Joe, but because of his prior experiences (with you and/or other individuals in a leadership role) or simply because he was having a bad day, he expressed a negative reaction to your greeting. Regardless, you are in discord.

Discord can also emerge during *focusing*. This can occur when an individual has multiple priorities and tasks at hand, and you as a leader prematurely choose one or more of these areas to focus on without adequately involving the individual in the agenda setting process. For example, Joe may be preoccupied with the fact that one of his team members is absent and he has a deadline approaching, while you may be focusing on today's optimistic quarterly sales report.

Discord can likewise emerge during the *evoking* process. As discussed previously, ambivalence is a natural part of the change process. If those you lead are ambivalent about a change, by definition they feel two ways about changing. They both want to change and don't want to. If we solely focus on evoking change talk, without ever acknowledging the individual's reluctance to change, we can inadvertently elicit discord. Consider the following example:

Leader: "So what reasons do you see for completing the upcoming communication skills training?"

Team Member: "Well, of course, anyone who's working directly with people needs to know how to communicate effectively. It's just, I've never had any formal complaints from other members of the team or the people we work with, I usually get really good feedback about the work I do with them, and I've just got too much on my plate at this time."

L: "What might make the training a higher priority for you at this time?"

T: "At this time? That's just it, now is not a good time. I could see doing it later; I suppose there's always room for improvement, and maybe the training could be useful. But now is not the best time. Perhaps after the end of the fiscal year when several of the current projects wrap up."

L: "It sounds like you recognize that the training could help you out some. How do you feel that may be the case?"

T: "Well, like I said, everyone could probably get better, but that's not really the issue."

L: "So nobody's perfect. Where do you see room for improvement for you?"

T: "I suppose I could learn to listen more effectively. As you know, my individual satisfaction ratings are pretty high across the board, but my ratings on the listening domain aren't as high as in the other domains."

L: "So you're seeing room for improvement in listening, and you see a role for the communication skills training in addressing that. Sounds like you're interested in attending the training next month."

T: "I don't think *you're* listening to *me*! While I think the training may be helpful, now's just not the right time. I mean, you're the leader, and I'll go if you make me, but you should know that if I go, I'm not going to be able to work on these other projects you said were so important."

Finally, discord can emerge during *planning*. Once the individual is ready, willing, and able to work on a particular change, it can be tempting as the leader to take off the MI hat and put on the expert hat. After all, you're the leader for a reason, and you know how to make change happen! However, even when the individual is ready for change, if the leader does not engage the individual in the planning process, he or she may balk at the plan, and the leader-led relationship can take a hit.

So how might you react when sustain talk or discord arises during one of the MI processes? The answer is, in short, that you build upon your OARS, using some specific strategies. Even though the strategies of responding to sustain talk and discord are very similar (with one notable exception described below), it is worth noting that the way we use each may vary somewhat depending on whether we're responding to sustain talk or discord.

To clarify, it is important to recognize what discord signifies: that is, a breakdown in the relationship between you and the other individual. Recall the four processes in MI-LEAD: engaging, focusing, evoking change talk, and planning. When discord emerges, re-engaging becomes the primary focus. That is, we need to return, at least temporarily, to the *engaging* process and rebuild trust and rapport. For this, our OARS, along with some other strategies, will be very important. Before we delve further into that, it is worth explicitly recognizing this important difference in responding to sustain talk and discord. With sustain talk, you may remain in the current MI process or perhaps revisit the previous process (for example, return to evoking before continuing to plan) until sustain talk starts to diminish and change talk emerges and/or strengthens. With discord, on the other hand, your primary goal is to first re-establish the relationship, which may involve returning to the engaging process before attempting to continue within the current process.

When you and your team member are moving through the processes of MI, namely engaging, focusing, evoking change talk, and eventually planning, recall the three-legged race. In your desire as a leader to get to planning, you may run ahead, leaving your team member behind you. This may lead to sustain talk or, even more significantly, to discord. When you as the dedicated leader pause to look, you may notice in this case that your team member is dragging along the ground behind you. In fact, your team member may be rather unhappy about your single-minded commitment to hurrying him across the finish line without fully appreciating where he is in the process, and discord may result.

Reflective Listening

So then, how do you use your OARS to respond to sustain talk and discord? Let's start with reflective listening. As we have indicated, this is the most important skill within MI-Lead in general, and it's no different when it comes to responding to sustain talk and discord in particular. There are, however, some specific types of reflections that can be especially useful in these situations. First is the *double-sided reflection*, which, as the name suggests, reflects both sides of the person's ambivalence. These can be used to respond to sustain talk ("Part of you wants to throw in the towel on the project, and another part really wants to see it through to the end.") or discord ("You're frustrated at me for pushing you on this, and you're looking for ways we can work together.").

The use of "and" instead of "but" in the above examples is intentional, as is the order in which both sides of the ambivalence are reflected. *And* recognizes that both sides of the ambivalence can co-exist, whereas *but* negates what was initially said. Think of "but" as a giant eraser; it erases everything that you said prior to the "but." Consider your reaction to the following statement, "You've been doing some great work recently, but you have been getting a late start in the mornings." What do you hear? Most would agree that the message that sticks is the one that follows the "but." The "great work that you've" done recently tends to get lost.

As for the order of the double-sided reflection, it is helpful to know that human beings tend to respond to the most recent thing that they heard. So, if we want those we lead to engage in change talk, or in talk about the benefits of making a particular choice, we will want to end our reflection with change talk ourselves. Let's look at two possibilities for making a double-sided reflection in response to the following statement by a team member when the goal is to improve collaboration by employees on projects, "I hate the way he always comes in at the last minute to fix a final programming glitch and then he seems to get all the credit for the entire, amazing project." Consider what the team member is likely to continue talking about if you reflect, "You are glad that the programming problems are solved so that the project can be completed, but it's unfair for someone else to get all the credit." In this case, it is likely that he will tell you more about his frustrations with someone else taking credit for an entire team's work. The conversation is likely to continue to remain focused on the inequity of stolen credit rather than on the great work of an entire team.

Now, consider the following reflection instead, "It is unfair to give only one person credit for a job well-done by many, and you and your colleagues are really proud of the work your team has produced." Chances are, your team member will share more about his and his colleagues' great work on this project. Your reflection has just elicited change talk and more change talk is related to an increased likelihood for change!

Keeping this point in mind, a straightforward, single-sided reflection of what the individual said can also be useful, as it demonstrates in a validating manner that you heard and understood what the person said. However, we see limited utility in using this with sustain talk (that is, only reflecting sustain talk), as, even though it is likely to engage, it is unlikely to elicit change talk. The notable exceptions to the use of reflecting sustain talk are during the engaging process (when you haven't even explicitly determined a focus yet and, thus, may not be fully aware of what sustain talk even is) or during evoking when all you seem to be getting is sustain talk, despite your best efforts to elicit change talk. When the latter happens, a useful strategy can be to summarize all the sustain talk you've heard, in order to demonstrate that you truly understand where the individual is coming from, and then immediately attempt to elicit change talk with a reflection or open-ended question. For example, "It sounds like you don't really see the point of working on developing the new program, especially as you think there's an already-developed program out there that does what we need. You also see this work as potentially taking a lot more time than we're anticipating, and you're concerned that it will take you away from other priorities. I'm wondering what potential *benefits* you may see in moving forward on the program, if any?"

Straightforward reflections can be especially useful when discord is present, as they help to engage with the individual and (re)establish the relationship. Reflections of the individual's emotions ("You're really frustrated by this.") and/or of the perceived rift in the relationship ("You think I'm being totally unreasonable right now.") can be especially useful, as they serve to recognize the issue at hand and set the tone for a productive, non-defensive discussion.

Another useful type of reflection in responding to sustain talk and discord is *reframing*. Reframing is finding the underlying positive connotation in an otherwise negative statement and reflecting this back to the individual. This can be used effectively with both sustain talk and discord, as demonstrated in the two examples below.

T: I don't think I can do this. I've tried like a hundred times, and I just can't get it. [Sustain talk]

L: You're really determined to figure this out.

T: I'm not really getting anywhere on this, and your riding my back isn't helping at all. [Sustain talk and Discord]

L: In order to make any sort of progress, you need some space.

It may go without saying that, in order for reframing to be effective, it must be done genuinely and accurately. In other words, if it comes across as fake, off-target, or overly effusive, it is likely to generate additional sustain talk or discord.

An *overshoot* is a type of reflection that intentionally exaggerates an individual's sustain talk or discord statement in an attempt to have the person move away from his or her initial statement. It is one of the rare times within MI–Lead that we, as leaders, are trying to be *inaccurate* with our reflections. By going to the extreme, we hope the individual moves in the opposite direction. Quite often, this is the case.

T: I don't think I can do this. I've tried like a hundred times, and I just can't get it. [Sustain talk]

L: You don't believe there is any possibility at all that you could figure this out. [Overshoot]

T: Well, I wouldn't go that far. I mean, if I had more time, and maybe a little more support, I might be able to make some progress. [Ability change talk]

L: So you've got some hope. What would that additional support look like?

Sometimes, however, what we hope to be an overshoot turns out to be an accurate reflection. While this is not the ideal response, it is nonetheless useful information, as it gives us a meaningful indication of the individual's level of readiness for change with regard to the current behavioral target(s). In which case, the discussion may shift to another behavioral target (that is, re-focus) or to planting seeds for future change around the current target behavior (see example below as well as the following section on *hypothetical questions* for more on this).

T: I don't think I can do this. I've tried like a hundred times, and I just can't get it. [Sustain talk]

L: You don't believe there is any possibility at all that you could figure this out. [Overshoot]

T: Right. I've already put 20 hours into this and have made absolutely zero progress. I need to move on to something else. [More sustain talk]

L: Now's not the time. What would need to be in place for you to come back to this later? [Simple reflection and open-ended question]

T: I don't know. I think I just need to focus on something else right now and let this simmer on the back burner. Maybe coming back to it later after working on something else would give me a fresh perspective. [More sustain talk along with some change talk]

L: You feel like you would be more effective on this project if you took some time away from it and worked on something else for a while. What do you think would be helpful to work on in the meantime? [Simple reflection, representing *coming alongside*, and open-ended question]

The example above starts with an attempted overshoot, which turns out instead to be an accurate reflection. The individual is indicating a lack of interest in continue working on the current project at this time. We might try probing a little more around this with additional reflections (perhaps a double-sided reflection) or other OARS. Once we're sure that the individual is truly not ready to work on the current change behavior, we might try a reflection that involves *coming alongside*. That is, a reflection that acknowledges and accepts the person's current lack of readiness to change. This reflection might also include any change talk from the individual regarding what would have to be in place in order to work on the project at a later time. Coming alongside allows you to minimize additional sustain talk or discord (by avoiding butting heads through pushing hard for change around the current behavior), helps plant seeds for future change around the target behavior, and sets the stage (along with an open-ended question) for eliciting the individual's ideas around target behaviors that he or she *is* ready to work on at this time. The final leader responses in the above example attempts to accomplish each of these goals.

Open-Ended Questions

As you can see in the above examples, *open-ended questions* can be used in conjunction with reflections to respond effectively to sustain talk and discord, although it is perhaps worth repeating that reflective listening is the single most important skill when responding to these types of statements. Leaders can respond quite effectively to sustain talk and discord through the use of reflections alone. Prior to using open-ended questions, we would suggest that you consider reflecting first, especially when it comes to discord. As we have previously noted, open-ended questions are a wonderful tool for eliciting the individual's ideas, particularly around a particular change. If discord is present, immediately attempting to elicit talk about change or about addressing the discord can be off-putting without first acknowledging the discord. Consider the following example:

T: I'm not really getting anywhere on this, and you riding my back isn't helping at all. [Sustain talk and discord]

L: What *would* help you to move forward? [Open-ended question]

T: Well, *not* constantly looking over my shoulder and asking about my progress for starters. [More discord]

In this example, the open-ended question merely served to elicit additional discord. We could see this question working well, however, particularly if preceded by a reflection acknowledging the initial discord, as in the following example:

T: I'm not really getting anywhere on this, and you riding my back isn't helping at all. [Sustain talk and discord]

L: It feels like I'm constantly hovering around you, and that's not helpful at all. [Reflection]

T: Yeah, it's like I'm constantly updating you or worried that you're going to check in on me any second, and instead of actually working on the project, I'm trying to figure out what I'm going to tell you when you check in. [Sustain talk with less discord]

L: So, my checking in frequently isn't helping you get anywhere. What *would* help you to move forward? [Reflection and open-ended question]

T: Well, I know you need to know what kind of progress I'm making, especially with the deadline coming up. But maybe if you could check-in less frequently and did so at a specific time, like the end of the week. That way, I could spend most of my time working on the project, and then I could start working on the update right before we meet. [Change talk]

Of course, an open-ended question in absence of an initial reflection won't necessarily elicit additional discord or sustain talk, and adding an initial reflection won't guarantee the opposite. Nevertheless, we have found it quite helpful to reflect some aspect of the discord, whether it's the individual's feelings (such as frustration) or thoughts about the situation (including the individual's perception of our role in it), before attempting to engage with the individual around generating a solution.

When it comes to using open-ended questions in situations described above, we find two types of these questions to be particularly valuable. The first of these are questions that ask for elaboration, such as "What would that look like?" or "Tell me more about that" (while technically a command statement, we think of "Tell me more about that" as an open-ended question, or *open-ended inquiry*, because it serves the purpose of eliciting information within the MI spirit). Asking for elaboration, especially in the presence of discord, avoids defensiveness, the righting reflex, and, potentially, the escalation of discord. Instead, it implicitly acknowledges the presence of discord and encourages further discussion of it within a collaborative framework. Instead of minimizing, ignoring, defending, or otherwise running away from the problem, you are acknowledging it and demonstrating an inquisitive nature around it, thus creating an atmosphere that encourages positive problem-solving.

T: I'm not really getting anywhere on this, and your riding my back isn't helping at all. [Sustain talk and discord]

L: It sounds like I'm doing more harm than good by checking in on you. Tell me more about that. [Reflection and open-ended inquiry]

T: Well, it's not that you're checking in on me—I know you need updates from time to time. It's just that I never know when you're going to stop by, and it seems like you're doing it even more often as the deadline approaches. I mean, I understand why, but I feel like I'm spending more time trying to figure out what I'm going to tell you when you check in than I am on actually working on the project. Maybe if we could just set up a time for me to report out, like at the weekly team meeting, and just stuck with that time, I could spend more time working on the project and less time looking over my shoulder or thinking about what to report. [Sustain talk and change talk]

L: Having me check in frequently isn't really helping. At the same time, you know I need the updates, and you feel like you could be more productive if this was done less frequently and at a time you knew in advance. [Double-sided reflection]

T: Exactly! That way I could spend more time working and less time worrying. [Change talk]

It may go without saying that asking for elaboration around sustain talk will encourage additional sustain talk. Generally we attempt to elicit change talk and minimize sustain talk; however, in limited circumstances (such as during the *engaging* process), elaborating around sustain talk may be beneficial. Asking for elaboration can be useful for addressing discord, and it is especially useful for reinforcing and encouraging additional change talk, but it has limited utility in responding to sustain talk.

A second type of open-ended question that can be especially useful in responding to discord and/or sustain talk is the *hypothetical question*. As noted in the previous chapter, hypothetical questions involve asking the individual to consider a change without having to commit to it. This can help free the individual of any constraints or barriers around the current set of circumstances, whether real or perceived, and instead focus on what successfully changing might look like. Here are some examples of hypothetical questions:

- *"If you were able to make this change, what would that look like?"*

- *"If you did feel it was important to meet this deadline, how might you go about doing so?"*

- *"If you had any resources available, how might you go about this in order to succeed?"*

- *"What could you do to complete this project, if anything were possible?"*

- *"What could you see me doing in order to be more helpful for you?"*

- *"If you and I were to start over, with an eye toward success, how might we do things differently?"*

- *"If you could wave a magic wand and make this barrier go away, how would that change things?"*

Asking an individual a hypothetical question can reduce sustain talk and discord because it does not put any pressure on the person to change. Instead, it frees the individual to envision change without constraint or commitment. *Without pressure, there is no need to defend.* With this freedom, when using hypothetical questions to respond to *sustain talk*, the individual is likely to provide change talk. When using these questions to respond to *discord*, the individual is likely to offer ideas about improving the current relationship. Because of the nature of these types of questions, the individual's response may contain elements of the fanciful or otherwise unrealistic. Even so, the person's response may also include elements or themes that are relevant or practical, and these are worth reflecting and having the individual elaborate upon further.

T: "I don't think I can do this. I've tried like a hundred times, and I just can't get it." [Sustain talk]

L: "You don't believe there is any possibility at all that you could figure this out." [Overshoot]

T: "Right. I've already put 20 hours into this and have made absolutely zero progress. I need to move on to something else." [More sustain talk]

L: "It's certainly sounding that way. Before we move on, though, I'm wondering…if you *were* to continue working on this, what would have to be in place?" [Reflection and hypothetical question]

T: "Well, if I could meet with the guy who invented this program, and pick his brain, then maybe I could get an idea of how to go forward." [Change talk]

L: "So, if you had an expert to consult with, someone who knows this program inside and out, then you could see maybe sticking with it for a little longer." [Reflection]

T: "It's possible. I certainly can't get any further on my own." [Change talk along with sustain talk]

The conversation can now shift to problem-solving around finding an expert consultant, or, if this is not practical, and another solution around overcoming the barrier is not forthcoming, the conversation may need to shift towards the individual moving on to another project for now. Either way, the hypothetical question can allow for some creative brainstorming that may yield an actionable solution.

Affirmations

Affirmations also serve a useful role in the current context. Recognizing the individual's strengths, efforts, commitment, values, goals, and/or intentions can improve both the motivations to change and your relationship with the individual. So, how can you use affirmations to respond to sustain talk or discord?

Often, hidden amongst the sustain talk or discord coming from the individual, there are hints, implications, glimpses, or even outright statements of change. Where the person voices doubt, we hear hope. What some may see as stubbornness, we see as determination and "stick-to-itness." The key to affirmations is the ability to find and highlight the positive and to do so in a genuine and relevant manner. This can be particularly challenging for at least a couple of reasons.

First, chances are that you have become a leader in part because of your problem-solving skills. You are a fixer, and you work by the motto, *Find It, Fix It!* As such, it is difficult to re-orient towards the positive in the presence of a problem. So, when an individual approaches you with one, the tendency is to immediately jump into problem-solving mode. In other words, for problem-solvers, the default response to sustain talk and/or discord is the righting reflex. The second challenge around affirming the positive is related to the first; we actually have to actively listen for the positive and tune our minds toward change talk. This can be especially challenging in the presence of discord, which often pushes our buttons and pulls for defensiveness or even going on the offense.

Instead, we encourage listening for signs or utterances of strengths, efforts, commitment, values, goals, and/or intentions in the individual's speech and then reflecting these back. This may come about as a *reframe*, as in the reframing examples presented earlier in the chapter, or it may be another type of reflection of something positive said or inferred. As noted above, the key here is to do so in a manner that is genuine, not contrived or "cheerleady," and relevant to the discussion at hand. Irrelevant or overly general affirmations ("You can do it!") are rarely as useful as more relevant and specifics ones ("Despite these setbacks, you're determined to see this through to the end.").

Summaries

Remember, summaries are a series of reflections of what the individual has previously stated. They can include sustain talk, change talk, or any other talk uttered by the individual, and the ratio of these is completely up to you. In other words, more than half the statements from the individual, up until this point, may have been sustain talk, but in your summary you can choose to mostly highlight change talk.

L: "So what reasons do you see for completing the upcoming communication skills training?"

T: "Well, of course, anyone who's working directly with people needs to know how to communicate effectively. It's just, I've never had any formal complaints from other members of the team or the people we work with, I usually get really good feedback about the work I do with them, and I've just got too much on my plate at this time."

L: "What might make the training a higher priority for you at this time?"

T: "At this time? That's just it, now is not a good time. I could see doing it later; I suppose there's always room for improvement, and maybe the training could be useful. But now is not the best time. Perhaps after the end of the fiscal year when several of the current projects wrap up."

L: "It sounds like you recognize that the training could help you out some. How do you feel that may be the case?"

T: "Well, like I said, everyone could probably get better, but that's not really the issue."

L: "So nobody's perfect. Where do you see room for improvement for you?"

T: "I suppose I could learn to listen more effectively. As you know, my individual satisfaction ratings are pretty high across the board, but my ratings on the listening domain aren't as high as in the other domains."

L: "You're seeing possibility for improvement in listening, and you're thinking some additional training in this area could be helpful. So where do we go from here?"

T: "Well, like I said, I think some training could be helpful, but the timing is all wrong. I have too many deadlines coming up as it is, and even if you made me go to the training next month I don't think I could concentrate enough to get anything from it. I just need to focus on getting my work done for now and worry about improving my communication skills later, especially since my ratings in this area are already so good."

L: "So, it sounds like you're feeling pretty good about your overall communication skills at this time, and your primary focus is on wrapping up a few projects by the end of the fiscal year. At the same time, you're recognizing that listening more effectively is a area of improvement for you, you're seeing potential value in being able to improve in this area, and you think some additional training may be useful. You appreciate that we're offering the training to staff, and you're thinking that participating in the training sometime after the start of the next fiscal year might be a good idea."

T: "Yeah, my plate will be mostly clean then, and a change of pace might be nice."

As with double-sided reflections, it's worth pointing out that the order and weight of the statements you reflect are very important. If your summary is more heavily weighted towards sustain talk, and especially if it ends on sustain talk, you are more likely to hear additional sustain talk from the person. If you want to instead elicit change talk, and we hope that we have convinced you at this point that you do, you might consider including a higher ratio of change talk relative to sustain talk in your summary and ending on the former.

The same is true in your response to discord. In your conversation with an individual around discord up until this point, you've heard statements around concerns, dissatisfaction, etc. with your relationship, the organization, and/or some other aspect of the situation. If you've used some of the strategies outlined above and elsewhere in this book, you've likely also heard what the individual values, appreciates, or otherwise feels is important about the relationship with you and/or current situation. When summarizing, it is useful to highlight the latter by giving it more "airtime" and ending on it.

L: "Part of you feels like I'm riding your back when it comes to getting updates. Another part recognizes that I need to know where you are on the project, especially with the deadline approaching. You see a potential compromise, one that involves you updating me without having to constantly worry about me showing up out of the blue. Going forward, you feel like the most effective approach would be for you to report out at scheduled intervals."

Honoring Autonomy

Sometimes we get sustain talk and discord because the other individual feels there were no other options or choices in the change process, that the individual has no say in the "how", "what", or "why" of change. Of course, this is simply not accurate. While we can certainly make it uncomfortable for the individual to exert autonomy, we cannot prevent the individual from doing so. And why would we want to? Given what we know about effective leadership, particularly in light of the research summarized in Chapter One, we want to encourage the person's right to choose. In fact, we want to explicitly acknowledge that choice. Doing so when someone is feeling as though their autonomy is being compromised can be particularly useful, as it serves to empower the individual and (re)establish the collaborative process.

Here's an example of responding to employee sustain talk by honoring autonomy:

T: "I'm not sure that I can take on another project at this time."

L: "If it's OK, I'd like to share with you some information about the organization's top priorities at this time and where the various projects we're all working on fit in with these. Ultimately, though, what you choose to work on is up to you."

Here's another example, this time of honoring autonomy in response to discord:

T: "I'm sick of being micro-managed! I know you're my boss and all, but that doesn't give you the right to tell me what to do and how to do it. Your job is to tell me the goal and then get out of my way so I can reach it."

L: "You're right, what you choose to do is up to you. I can share with you the pros and cons of what you decide to do, if you like, but I can't make you do anything."

It is important to note that we are not suggesting that there are no negative consequences (for example, loss of job, demotion, reassignment, loss of bonus, performance improvement plan, etc.) for the individual's choices nor that we should ignore such consequences. What we *are* suggesting is that, despite such consequences, it is the person's right to choose what they do, and that emphasizing this choice engages and empowers a person and makes positive change more likely than when that individual feels powerless.

Apologizing

Each of the strategies presented above can be used effectively with both sustain talk and discord, although keep in mind the limited utility of simple reflections in response to sustain talk. Apologizing, on the other hand, only makes sense in response to discord. With sustain talk, there is nothing for which you need to apologize. While you may be unhappy or disappointed with someone's lack of importance or confidence around engaging in some change, what, exactly, do you have to apologize for? Go ahead and try it out mentally. How do you imagine the individual might respond to your following statement: "I'm sorry that you don't find the current project more important." As you imagine her response, is it one of increasing hope, desire, ability, or commitment around change? Chances are, you're instead envisioning defensiveness, statements of inability, reasons why now is not the time, or incompatible prioritization. In other words, you're expecting sustain talk.

With discord, however, apologizing can be an important step toward (re)establishing the relationship. As Miller and Rollnick state, "This costs you nothing and immediately acknowledges that this is a collaborative relationship" (2013). In other words, it puts the relationship between you and the individual front and center, highlighting the importance of it. As noted with other strategies above, this should be used only when felt genuinely and within the spirit of MI. It hopefully goes without saying that if used as an attack (whether backhanded or forward) against the individual ("I'm sorry that you don't have the wherewithal to figure this out."), the apology will likely cause more discord. However, when used genuinely, and when you truly feel you (or the team or organization you represent) has a role to play in the situation contributing to discord, apologizing can be a powerful harmonizing force.

L: "So you're seeing room for improvement in listening, and you see a role for the communication skills training in addressing that. Sounds like you're interested in attending the training next month."

T: "I don't think *you're* listening to *me*! While I think the training may be helpful, now's just not the right time. I mean, you're my boss, and I'll go if you make me, but you should know that if I go, I'm not going to be able to work on these other projects you said were so important."

L: "I think I got a little bit ahead of you there. Sorry about that. It sounds like you're seeing some potential value in the training, but not now. Once you take care of some more pressing issues, you might consider it then."

Chapter Summary

Sustain talk is normal and natural and likely to surface from those you lead when they are ambivalent about, or otherwise not ready for, change. Discord is a breakdown in the relationship between you and the individual and can "meet you at the door" or emerge from the way you interact with the person. Left unaddressed, both sustain talk and discord are indicators that positive change is not imminent. How we respond to sustain talk and discord plays an important part in whether these behaviors increase or decrease in magnitude and frequency. In this chapter, we discussed how certain leadership behaviors (the righting reflex, in particular) are likely to cause increased sustain talk and discord, while other behaviors (such as OARS, honoring autonomy, and apologizing) are likely to minimize sustain talk and discord and make positive change more likely. We provided several examples of sustain talk and discord as well as effective and ineffective leadership response to each. Finally, we conclude the chapter with an opportunity to further practice identifying sustain talk and discord and responding effectively to each.

Exercise 8.1

For each example below, read the statement and identify whether it includes sustain talk, discord, or a combination of the two. The context of the conversation is that you are discussing a number of tasks that you would like someone you lead to work on, such as completing a report, consistently arriving on time, and orienting a new team member.

1. *"I just don't have the time to work on this right now."*

2. *"It's really hard for me to get to work on time when I can't drop the kids off at school any earlier than 7:45 every morning, especially when traffic is so bad at that time."*

3. *"You're being totally unreasonable."*

4. *"I can finish the report or I can work with our new team members, but I can't do both. If you worked with us in the trenches, you would realize this."*

5. *"I'm not really that good at orienting new team members. Hiro's really much better at that. Can you ask him instead?"*

6. *"I wish you'd quit bugging me about the report. I'll get to it when I get to it."*

7. *"I know I need to finish the report, it's just with everything else going on, I don't think I'll meet the deadline."*

8. *"I don't see what the big deal is about getting here right at 8:00 am every morning. You know I stay late every night and put in way more than 40 hours each week. So what's the big deal?"*

9. *"Can't we talk about this later? I've got bigger fish to fry at the moment."*

10. *"I'm not sure I understand the purpose of the report. It seems like every time I complete and submit it, it just gets rewritten. Is it really so important that I submit it, when the end product looks nothing like what I wrote? Wouldn't my time be better spent elsewhere?"*

Answers
1. Sustain talk
2. Sustain talk
3. Discord
4. Sustain talk and discord
5. Sustain talk
6. Discord
7. Sustain talk
8. Sustain talk and discord
9. Sustain talk (and possibly discord, depending on tone in which the statement and question are made)
10. Sustain talk

Exercise 8.2

This time, for each of the same statements as above, come up with a response that is likely to reduce the sustain talk and/or discord. The context of the conversation is the same as above.

1. *"I just don't have the time to work on this right now."*

_____
_____

2. *"It's really hard for me to get to work on time when I can't drop the kids off at school any earlier than 7:45 every morning, especially when traffic is so bad at that time."*

_____
_____

3. "You're being totally unreasonable."

4. "I can finish the report **or** I can work with our new team members, but I can't do both. If you worked with us in the trenches, you would realize this."

5. "I'm not really that good at orienting new team members. Hiro's really much better at that. Can you ask him instead?"

6. "I wish you'd quit bugging me about the report. I'll get to it when I get to it."

7. "I know I need to finish the report, it's just with everything else going on, I don't think I'll meet the deadline."

8. "I don't see what the big deal is about getting here right at 8:00 am every morning. You know I stay late every night and put in way more than 40 hours each week. So what's the big deal?"

9. *"Can't we talk about this later? I've got bigger fish to fry at the moment."*

10. *"I'm not sure I understand the purpose of the report. It seems like every time I complete and submit it, it just gets re-written. Is it really so important that I submit it, when the end product looks nothing like what I wrote? Wouldn't my time be better spent elsewhere?"*

Possible answers:

1. *"Sounds like now's not the time for you to work on this. When do you see the time being right?"* [Straightforward reflection and open-ended question]

    "In order to work on this project right now, some other things would have to change." [Complex reflection]

2. *"You'd really like to figure this out."* [Complex reflection]

    "You don't see any possible solution." [Overshoot]

3. *"You're concerned that I don't get it."* [Straightforward reflection]

    "You're not sure we'll ever be able to see eye-to-eye on this." [Overshoot]

4. *"You think I'm being unreasonable."* [Straightforward reflection]

"You feel if I was more aware of your actual demands I could give you better direction, which is what you're looking for." [Complex reflection]

5. *"You'd rather work on what you're best at for now. If you were to help out with orienting new team members in the future, what would need to happen to get you feeling comfortable with this role?"* [Straightforward reflection and hypothetical question]

"In order to be involved in orienting new team members, you feel you would need to get better at this task. What can we do to help with this?" [Complex reflection and open-ended question]

6. *"I apologize if I've been too overbearing about this. Sounds like you have a plan for going forward on this on your own."* [Apology and complex reflection]

"You don't need anything else from me right now; you've got everything you need to get the report done on time." [Reframe]

7. *"What can I do to help?"* [Open-ended question]

"You know this is important, and you're looking for some ideas on how you might accomplish this task." [Complex reflection]

8. *"You want to make sure that I see you are committed to the team."* [Complex reflection]

"You certainly are putting in the work, and it shows! I wonder if you might see any potential downsides to coming in after 8:00 am on some mornings?" [Affirmation and hypothetical question]

9. *"You're overwhelmed at the moment. When would be a better time this morning for us to discuss this?"* [Complex reflection and open-ended question]

   "You're feeling unable to focus on what I have to discuss right now unless it's an even bigger fish." [Reframe]

10. *"In order to feel like your time is being well-spent in this process, you need to better understand the value of your contributions."* [Complex reflection]

    "You're a team player and want to make sure that whatever you're doing is contributing to the mission of the team." [Affirmation]

Chapter 9

Planning: How does it fit?

In this chapter, we will discuss how to go about planning with those you lead. This entails defining the vision or big picture, identifying clear and concise long-term goals, and creating specific and realistic short-term goals. We will go over some tools that will assist you and your teams in achieving success in each of these areas. In doing so, we'll revisit the Elicit, Provide, Elicit (EPE) strategy for sharing information and discuss its application in planning.

In Chapter Six, we talked about the four processes, with the fourth being the *Planning* process. Unlike the other three processes, planning isn't necessary in the practice of MI-Lead, but it can be a very important component. In the third edition of Motivational Interviewing, Miller and Rollnick give this description about the processes:

Engaging is about "Shall we travel together?"

Focusing asks "Where to?"

Evoking is about "Whether?" and "Why?" and

Planning is about "How?" and "When?"

As you transition into the planning process, helping and guiding individuals and teams to discover their "How" and "When" can make the difference between their being highly successful and their never even getting started. Before we discuss the specifics of planning within MI-Lead, let's discuss the importance of having a *vision*.

Vision - Big Picture

In a leadership position, it is important to have some type of *vision* or big picture perspective, and it is also important that you are able to convey this vision with clarity to others. This big picture perspective will help guide you and your team(s) in determining which projects to take on and how to implement them as well as in everyday decision-making. If you don't already have a sense of your organization's or team's vision or big picture perspective, it will be important to take the time to identify this "bird's-eye view", develop it, and be prepared to talk meaningfully about it with your team(s). Your vision may derive entirely from the larger organization's goals or it may be unique to your particular role within the organization. Regardless, there is value in being able to identify and articulate a "true north" that will provide direction to the actions of you and those you lead: a compass that orients all toward a common and valued destination. This will help provide clarity to those you lead, building trust in you as well as confidence and commitment to the goals. It will also provide a starting point, from which you and your team can develop a shared agenda or focus.

In some instances, you as a leader or manager may not know all of the details about a specific program and, if this is the case, you and your team may choose to work with the team or team lead to develop a clear idea of the vision or big picture. Of note, the vision is not the same as the long-term goal. It is the guide for the long-term goals. Consider the following example:

A program in a health care organization is trying to increase client adoption of healthier lifestyles. In this case, the organization's vision for what it hopes the program will accomplish is the following: "Our vision is to provide high quality, preventive health care that leads to a decrease in behaviorally based illnesses and unnecessary hospital admissions."

At times, the vision may be analogous to the organization's mission statement. Jason recalls that, during a recent training that he was facilitating, one of the participants asked the question, "Does anyone know what our mission statement is?" The group was silent; no one had an answer. The participant utilized this opportunity to share the company's mission statement and its importance. His passion about the company's mission was infectious and helped other participants to see the value in basing future decisions and actions on this mission. This leader's commitment to the vision was an important one; the mission statement for this organization gave direction for aligning actions and individual projects.

If you as the leader have identified the vision, which is likely the case, then your next step will be to share this vision with your team. Thinking about your own organization or team, once you have identified your group's mission or vision, how might you describe it in a sentence or two? Narrowing the focus to a manageable statement simplifies the next step, development of long-term goals.

Developing Long-Term Goals

Long-term goals ideally align with the vision, and, as a leader, it will be important for you to know how they are aligned. If your are not clear about the alignment between the overall vision for the group and the goals you develop to support that vision, it is unlikely that those you lead will appreciate the relationship between their goals and the "bigger picture." If those you lead don't understand the purpose in their tasks, it is unlikely that they will take ownership for their part in achieving the organizational goals.

Remembering the process of focusing in MI-Lead, the development of long-term goals is a collaborative effort among team members. As a leader, your communication of interest and curiosity as well as respect for team input increases the likelihood that individuals will share insights, concerns, and ideas about the goals. This open communication during the development of these goals is important, not simply for team member buy-in, but also because it provides you and your team the opportunity to collaboratively adjust these goals to make them more realistic and achievable.

Successful development of long-term goals involves several factors. One component of a well-developed long-term goal is that it is defined in measurable terms, allowing for feedback and process improvements. A long-term goal defined as, "Improve customer service," is extremely vague. However, a goal or endpoint that is defined as, "Improve customer service survey score of 58% to 78% by the end of quarter one" is defined clearly and success is measurable. Included in the specific and measurable goal (increasing the customer rating by 20 points) and the target date for completion (end of quarter one).

So, how do you develop a long-term goal? The first step is in determining how you will measure your outcome. The next step will be to define the targeted change in that outcome. In other words, what is it that you or others within the organization would like to improve, how might you measure it, and what is a realistic outcome to seek in what amount of time. Flexibility is key. The long-term goals are most likely to be achieved when your team either contributes to its development or has a role in adjusting it or redefining it to make it realistic and achievable. Team support for the long-term goal can mean the difference between success or failure of that goal.

When talking to your team about the long-term goal, there will be times that you have information to share. Sharing information is absolutely consistent with MI and can be achieved using the EPE approach we discussed earlier: Elicit, Provide, Elicit.

A review of how it works:

The first step is to Elicit from an individual or team what they already know and then ask permission before providing information. Asking permission to share information is an explicit way to support autonomy and is consistent with the spirit of MI-Lead. If we continue with our customer service example, the discussion might look like this.

Leader: "What do you know about the measures we use for customer service?" (Asking what they know)

Team Member: "We know that our customer service rating is at 58% right now."

L: "I'm glad you know the latest numbers. I've been looking at the numbers and working on setting a long-term goal that we can achieve. If it's okay with you, I would like to share what I've come up with." (Asking permission to share)

T: "Yes, definitely."

The next step is to Provide information, and *how* you provide the information determines whether or not it is consistent with MI-Lead. Providing information in third person, describing how others have done something or felt about something, allows an individual or team to consider the information while maintaining their autonomy to choose how to proceed. If you, as a leader, are providing ideas on what to do, it's a good idea to offer a few options to choose from, again explicitly supporting the individual or team's autonomy. It is also important to keep your information straightforward and concise, offering small amounts at a time. Providing too much information is likely to cause your staff's attention to drift and the most important point may be lost. Here's what that part of the discussion might look like.

L: "Thanks. After looking at where we are, I would like for us to set a long term goal to Improve our customer service rating from 58% to 78% by the end of quarter one."

You'll notice it is specific and concise, while being respectful of the individual or team.

The final step is to Elicit again. While it is tempting to Elicit and then Provide without the final Elicit, this second opportunity to check in and to find out what the team understands or hears is particularly important in the collaborative agenda setting process. Communicating that you value both your thoughts and their thoughts increases engagement and buy-in. The second Elicit is normally achieved using an open-ended question. Continuing with our example, this question might follow:

L: "How do you see this long term goal impacting your work?" or "What thoughts do you have about the long term goal?" or "How realistic do you feel this is keeping in mind where we are right now?"

The team's response will give you valuable insight into their views about the goal(s). Where are they in terms of Processes? Are you hearing change talk or sustain talk? Are they also at the discussion stage (evoking statements of desire, ability, reasons, or need) or the planning stage (statements of "how" and "when"), or do you need to take a step back and spend more time on engaging or focusing? This format will also give your team the opportunity to ask further questions, giving you a chance to clarify and potentially adjust your approach as well as your target.

Let's look at the format for sharing information one more time:

Step 1: Elicit

L: "With our customer service numbers at 58%, what do you think would be a realistic long term goal that we could set for this department?"

T: "We could maybe try to increase it by 10% to 15%."

L: "You see a 10-15% increase as being realistic."

T: (nods)

L: "May I share what I've been thinking as well?"

T: "Sure."

Step 2: Provide

L: "I've been thinking that a 20% increase might encourage us to stretch a bit but would also be realistic."

Step 3: Elicit

L: "What are your thoughts about shooting for 20% vs. a 10-15% increase? Again, the 20% is something I am thinking would benefit the company in terms of customer loyalty, but you know a great deal about the department's capabilities, and I value your insights."

Remember, it's important not to be completely entrenched in your selection of long term goals because if those you lead have a different but appropriate goal in mind and a rationale for that goal, then it will be important to honor their input and genuinely consider adjusting the goal to one that addresses the agendas of both you and the individual or team.

Short-Term Goals

Short-term goals are the action goals that will help your team achieve the long-term benchmarks. These goals define the specific steps that individuals and/or teams will take in developing and implementing the changes. Like long-term goals, short-term goals have some specific components.

Short-term goals are based on *actions* and *behaviors*. They lead to *more immediate outcomes* versus long term goals that are the more distal results of those immediate outcomes, actions, and behaviors. Similar to long-term goals, it is important that the immediate outcomes of short-term goals are also measurable. If an individual defines a short-term goal as, "Employees offering customer care will start smiling more," or "will make customers happy," the individual may find that assessing the success of these goals is challenging at best. Measuring the before and after frequency of smiling by employees would be an arduous task, and how might we objectively define and measure "happy"?

A more appropriate short term or action goal might look like this, "Customer service representatives will greet each customer with a smile, with a success rate defined as greeting new customers with a smile of at least 90% of the time, as assessed during regular supervisor observations three times per week. In this example, the short-term goal or action plan has a measurement (increasing the number of times the staff smile at customers to 90%), it has a behavior (greeting new customers with a smile), and it has a timeframe (measured three times per week).

Choosing a measure that is representative of the long-term goal is important. Consider situations in which your team has worked to meet the action goal without an accompanied commitment to the longer-term goal. For example, if your long-term goal is to increase customer satisfaction over the next quarter, a short term goal of greeting each new customer with a smile at least 90% of the time would probably be appropriate since it represents an important aspect of customer satisfaction. Often those you lead can offer valuable input about how to best measure the outcomes of the team's goals and, sometimes, identification of appropriate measures occurs through trial and error! Not only do those you lead have the potential to offer valuable input and feedback during the selection of goals, their input offers you as the leader a window into their thoughts about whether a specific goal is attainable. Without a sense that goals can be reached, individuals are unlikely to maintain motivation for the action, leading to frustration and eventual failure to meet the goal. In contrast, an individual or team that feels included in the goal development process is likely to take greater ownership for the success of that goal, to offer creativity and meaningful input and feedback along the way, and to assist in adjusting goals to be achievable and realistic. Again, using an MI-

Lead consistent approach to the development and follow-through of short and long- term goals leads to individual or team engagement, successful development of shared goals, meaningful discussion about those goals, and successful planning and implementation of those goals.

In the implementation of the action plan, feedback and goal adjustment are important. After the short-term goal is developed and implementation is underway, follow-up meetings provide an opportunity to check in with the team member's progress with the goals. In these meetings, you as the leader can continue to incorporate MI-Lead skills as outlined throughout this book. When examining potential barriers and seeking solutions, it remains important to guide staff versus directing them, eliciting solutions from the team members whenever possible, and limiting your suggestions to when the team is struggling to find solutions. While it may be tempting to be the one who sets action goals for the team or team member, remember, change talk is associated with target change follow-through, and your advice is not change talk! The key is to elicit change talk from the team or team member as much as possible.

When you do offer examples or suggestions, using the EPE format minimizes the chances you will appear directive and inadvertently elicit sustain talk (leading to a decreased likelihood of plan follow through). When offering suggestions (with permission), providing a menu of choices (easy, moderate, more difficult to employ) communicates your continued respect for the individual or team's autonomy. This respect accomplishes two goals: the individual or team will be encouraged to take more ownership for the plan once it's developed and they will be more likely to follow through with the chosen plan, since it was theirs.

Chapter Summary

As discussed at the beginning of this chapter, long term and short term goals are great strategies for successful planning and follow through. However, planning in its most basic form is simply looking for the "How" and "When." While planning may involve fully setting the "how" and "when" for a goal, this stage may only consist of brainstorming or the individual or team may not even get into process four; they may opt to finish that part on their own.

In order for it to be MI-Lead, the first three processes are necessary (engaging, focusing, evoking change talk), but the fourth process (planning), even though it can be highly effective and impactful, may not always occur with you or in a formalized way. Additionally, setting the goals may not apply to every leadership situation.

Exercise 9.1

Write down a long-term goal that is relevant to your work area. Take it to someone and see if it makes sense and is clear enough for the individual to feel they could make a plan to get there.

Ask yourself:

- What do you want the end outcome to be?
- What will the long-term goal be?
- How might you explain this clearly within a few simple sentences?
- What outline or graphic can be used to visualize the end point?

Exercise 9.2

Write a sample short-term and long-term goal using the scenarios provided or come up with some of your own with scenarios that are relevant to your work.

1. Customer service rating for the last three months: March 45%, April 43%, May 44%.

Long Term Goal:
_____
_____
_____

Short Term Goal:
_____
_____
_____

2. Shoe sales for the last three months: Dec. 74%, Jan. 60%, Feb. 58%.

Long Term Goal:
_____
_____
_____

Short Term Goal:
_____
_____
_____

3. Average time for installations: Dec. 45 min. Jan. 42 min Feb. 46 min (Target 15 minutes)

Long Term Goal:
_____
_____
_____

Short Term Goal:
_____
_____
_____

Chapter 10

Ethical Considerations

Up to this point we've been primarily focused on how to use MI in leadership situations, with additional discussion of why it might be useful to do so. What we've hinted at, but haven't yet fully addressed, is when it is appropriate to use MI in leadership situations, and when it isn't. MI is a powerful tool for fostering behavior change. As such, it can easily be misused by leaders to manipulate those they lead, especially in supervisor/employee situations, because of the power differential between leader and led. In this chapter, we discuss leadership situations where MI-Lead is appropriate as well as those in which the use of MI-Lead is not. We include examples and exercises around ethical and practical issues associated with the use of MI-Lead in several leadership scenarios.

At its heart, MI is a pro-social endeavor. That is, MI is about doing what's best for others and placing the needs of others at least on equal footing as, if not ahead of, our own. This is apparent in our discussion of the spirit of MI, which emphasizes *compassion* (acting in the best interest of the other); *acceptance* of the other's actions, beliefs, behaviors, worth, and autonomy; *partnering* up with the other as opposed to giving direction; and utilizing the other's strengths, experiences, ideas, and wisdom by *evoking* these from the person. The goal of MI is to help others change in a way that promotes their own welfare.

It should come as no surprise then that two guiding ethical principles of MI, which we also insist on in MI-Lead, are non-maleficence and beneficence. *Non-maleficence* is the idea of doing no harm. It is ensuring that whatever we are doing with the other person is in no way acting against his or her best interests. *Beneficence* goes a step beyond and actively seeks to promote the best interests of the other person. It is working to ensure that what we are doing with the other is providing some benefit to the individual.

So what should you do if the team member and you (as the leader) disagree about what is in his or her best interest? As in other applications of MI, this can be a difficult challenge within MI-Lead. It is also one that must be addressed and resolved before you, as the leader, can proceed with the ethical application of MI-Lead. Dr. Kersh reflects upon this question in the following scenarios:

Within the clinical setting, the decision as to whether the use of MI is in the patient's best interest, even when he or she may not initially agree with this decision, is often obvious. For instance, as a mental health provider, my patient, we'll call Jorge, may not initially agree that reducing or eliminating methamphetamine use is in his best interests, but the significant impact of this use on his vocational, social, cognitive, and financial well-being indicate that it would be unethical for me not to address this behavior. In this case, I can rest assured that the use of MI is ethical, despite initial disagreements around my and my patient's beliefs around what is in his best interests.

But what if my client, who married his high school sweetheart 20 years ago and never had a serious romantic relationship with anyone else, is now considering a divorce in order to "live life to the fullest" and engage in additional romantic experiences. Is my use of MI ethical (to guide towards either divorce or remaining in the marriage) in this situation? Does it matter that I, as the clinician, have very strong beliefs (one way or the other) about the institution of marriage? In this case, we would argue that, despite my beliefs, it is not objectively clear which behavioral choice (remaining married vs. divorce) is most likely to do no harm and promote the best interests of the patient. As such, we would consider the use of MI to be unethical. While application of much of the spirit would still be ethical, as well as the use of OARS to engage with the patient and help him explore his own goals, values, and pros and cons of change, guiding toward change in any particular direction would not be ethical. Thus, the use of the overall MI approach would not be ethical.

Within leadership situations, much as in the second clinical situation described above, non-maleficence and beneficence may not be entirely clear and objective. There will be times when we as leaders do not agree with our team members' decisions around what is in their best interest. So, how do we resolve this, and when is it okay to use MI in these situations? The short answer is that we believe it is appropriate to use MI with your team members to engage with them to explore their goals and values and seek areas of alignment between the goals you have for the team member (what you perceive to be in their best interest) and those of the team members themselves (what they perceive to be in their best interest). In other words, it is appropriate to apply MI spirit and skills in the engaging and focusing processes. However, unless and until you and the team members find alignment in goals—that is, come to an agreement around what's in their best interest—then using MI to proceed to the evoking and/or planning process would be considered unethical, regardless of whether you are convinced that you really do have the team member's best interests in mind. Ultimately, what is in their best interest is their decision to make.

So how do the concepts of non-maleficence and beneficence fit in with leadership? To some leaders, the spirit of MI and its underlying ethical principles would appear to run counter to their view of the primary goal of leadership, which is to push, dictate, and possibly manipulate those they lead to act in such a way as to meet the needs of the organization, team, and/or leader. We suspect many who fall into this camp are leaders from the Theory X perspective. Such leaders are not likely to adopt the MI-Lead model because they see that enhancing a person or team's input and autonomy, outside of possibly a few, trivial occasions (for example, what should the theme of our next office party be?) would lead to overall decreased productivity. Other leaders, especially those from the Theory Y and Z, Transformational Leadership, Lean Management, and Servant leadership camps, may see the potential benefit to organizational goals from adopting the MI-Lead model, but may have concerns about applying this approach across the board in leadership situations and may even envision leadership situations where adhering to the MI spirit and ethical principles are not possible. To these individuals, we present the following considerations.

What are some of the ethical considerations around the use of MI-Lead in leadership situations? Miller and Rollnick (2013) discuss several such considerations when applying MI in general, and two of these strike us as especially relevant for leadership applications. First, the application of MI can be particularly problematic when the presence or appearance of *coercive power* is involved. That is, if an individual or team perceives (correctly or not) that the leader holds coercive power over them, then MI-Lead must be used by the leader judiciously, if at all. In such situations, the individual or team's feelings about the negative consequences of disagreeing with the leader (such as being fired, pushed out, let go, demoted, or overlooked) or the positive consequences of agreeing with the leader (such as ingratiating him or herself to the leader and/or enhancing potential for advancement or more favorable duties) may override the ability of the leader to truly honor the spirit of partnership, evocation, and acceptance. Since leadership positions often do involve the potential for coercive power, with less formal leadership positions (such as team leader for a temporary working group) involving some amount of implicit power, many leadership situations are fraught with the potential to misuse MI-Lead.

A similar area of concern is situations involving leadership *investment* in outcome of an individual's behaviors. These are situations in which the organization, team, and/or leader has a significant stake in the team member's behavior and, thus, is tempted to sway the individual's behavior in a particular direction. In such situations, the potential to misuse MI-Lead is considerable, and it becomes difficult to truly honor acceptance, evocation, partnership, and compassion. Because MI-Lead works, the temptation for the leader may be to use the skills and techniques to simply get the individual to do what the leader wants, not to promote the person's best interest or otherwise honor the MI spirit.

Since leadership situations often involve both investment and the potential for coercive power, when is MI-Lead *ever* appropriate to use in such situations? Simply put, MI-Lead is appropriate to use when the MI spirit, including the ethical principles noted above, can be honored. Below we outline several general situations where we believe the MI spirit cannot be honored and therefore advocate that the use of MI-Lead would be inappropriate. We also discuss situations where the use of certain MI processes (such as focusing or evoking) would not be appropriate whereas the implementation of others might be especially useful.

So when is it inappropriate to use MI-Lead in leadership situations? As implied above, MI-Lead is not appropriate to use in situations where the spirit of MI cannot be honored. In general, we see the following leadership situations as falling into this category:

- When using MI-Lead would cause harm or not be in the best interests of those you lead.

- When you are unaware of the team member's best interests or you and those you lead do not agree on their best interests.

- When you cannot honor the team member's choices (for instance, the individual ultimately has no say in the decision-making process).

- When you have significant personal (or organizational) investment in a particular outcome and intend to use your power as a leader to achieve it, regardless of the team member's preferences or needs.

In these types of situations, it becomes impossible to give anything more than "lip service" to such approaches as partnership, acceptance, compassion, and/or evocation. For instance, if you plan to follow a certain course of action regardless of what the team member or team wants to do, using MI-Lead in an attempt to get them to align with your goals without any openness to a change in plans on your own part would be an unethical application of MI-Lead.

Having said that, we see the core skills of MI (that is, OARS) as being almost universally applicable across leadership situations. So how do we explain the apparent contradiction? The answer lies in the intended purpose or goal of the application of MI skills in any particular situation. That is, it may be appropriate to use OARS to *engage* with someone you lead in a particular situation, such as when trying to learn what an individual's goals and values are (that is, what a team member sees as his or her best interests), while attempting to *evoke* a particular behavior from the individual in the same situation (for instance, in the absence of knowing his or her best interests) would be inappropriate. In other words, the determination of whether the use of MI-Lead is appropriate in any given leadership situation depends largely upon which MI process you are employing given the context of the situation. It may be that the general MI-Lead approach is appropriate, although given the current circumstances, one or more of the processes would be inappropriate from an ethical standpoint. Let us consider the following examples.

- *Engaging or focusing when the team member is ready for action in an appropriate direction.* In this scenario, the team member is ready to engage in an action plan that both you and the individual agree is in his or her best interest. For the leader, to operate from the *engaging* or *focusing* perspective could be counter-productive and impede the team member's progress toward effective behavior. The most ethical and effective approach in this case, once you are certain that your team member is committed to move forward toward a mutually-shared goal, would be to assist the team member in *planning* an effective strategy. To remain in the *engaging* or *focusing* process at this point would violate the MI ethical principles of non-maleficence and beneficence, as it would potentially interfere with your team member moving toward behavior change.

- *Evoking or planning when the leader's and employee's best interests are not in alignment.* Unlike the previous example, where the leader is lagging behind the employee, the current scenario is an example of the leader getting too far ahead of the employee. The most common example of this scenario is that the leader is motivated toward a particular goal and either assumes an employee shares the same goal or is indifferent as to whether the employee does so. In this case, to operate from the *evoking* or *planning* perspective, without first ensuring that the leader and the employee share the same goals and ideas around a particular target behavior, is to violate the basic MI spirit of compassion, acceptance, and partnering. The more ethical approach for the leader in this situation would be *engaging* and, once engagement is in place, *focusing*. Only when you are certain that you and your employee are in agreement around a behavioral target that is in the individual's best interest would it be ethically appropriate to operate from the *evoking* or *planning* perspective.

- *A decision by leadership has been made and the team member has very little, or no, say in the decision-making process, such as in disciplinary action or a performance improvement plan.* Again, as in the previous example, engaging might be an appropriate approach here. You may even find that by adopting the MI spirit and the engaging approach, the team member recognizes the need for action you and/or the organization has decided is necessary. In which case (that is, you both agree that the goal is in the team member's best interest), you may even see opportunity for team member input around the specific plan, in which case focusing, evoking, and planning could be appropriate. If, on the other hand, the team member actually does not have a say in the ultimate plan, the appearance of choice and input inherent in *focusing*, *evoking*, and *planning* would be illusory and, thus, ethically inappropriate.

- *A leader is invested in a particular outcome and intends to use coercive power to achieve it.* This is similar to previous examples, although it is hard to envision a case in this scenario where the use of any MI process is appropriate. Again, while we see the foundational skills of MI as being almost universally applicable across leadership situations, if the leader intends to move the team toward a particular action plan "by any means necessary," then the use of MI-Lead is categorically unethical as the leader is unable to fully honor the MI spirit. To engage, focus, evoke, or plan when you have absolutely no latitude around the ultimate action plan again makes the appearance of team member acceptance, choice, input, and empowerment a sham. If you have strong investment in a particular outcome *and* are willing to consider team member participation in the decision-making processes (including whether or not to participate at all), then MI-Lead might be appropriate. In such instances, the use of engaging and focusing can help ascertain whether the team member is truly on board or whether the individual is simply agreeing in order to avoid the negative consequences of disagreeing with the leader.

The above are a few examples of situations where the use of MI-Lead, or at least certain MI processes, would be considered unethical. To further develop our understanding of the ethical application of MI-Lead in leadership situations, consider the ethical issues associated with the use of MI-Lead in each of the following scenarios. Which, if any, of the MI processes would be appropriate for each of the scenarios?

1. Your team has been stagnating on a particular project for weeks, with little to no progress occurring on the project during that time. You feel that the team members have all

the resources they need to complete the project, if only they would commit to it.

2. You have a project deadline and you need someone you lead to complete a task in order to meet the deadline.

3. Your bonus, award, or other gain is dependent on completing a project by a certain deadline, and you need all team members to increase their productivity. Team members will not directly (that is, extrinsically) benefit from meeting the deadline.

4. Your supervisor or leader has assigned your team a project that, if successful, will increase profits or other benefits for the organization but will not directly benefit you, your team, or your organization's customers. Your team is already feeling overwhelmed by current projects and would have to work overtime (without additional compensation) in order to complete the project. Every team member has expressed resentment about getting this new project "tossed into our laps."

5. Your team is ready to get started on a project and has already mapped out a plan for initial steps that appears reasonable to all involved, including you. Every member of the team has identified both internal and external reasons for working on the project and has expressed excitement around being involved. If successful, the project would be beneficial to the team, you, the organization, and its stakeholders.

Let's tackle these one at a time. Does MI-Lead seem like an appropriate fit for Scenario #1? What ethical issues might be involved in this scenario? From our standpoint, we see this as being a great opportunity for using MI-Lead. It appears that the team is stuck despite having what they need to move forward, which might be an indication of ambivalence on the part of one or more team members. If this is indeed the case, trying to push the team forward through threat of punishment or promise of reward may not be all that effective. Instead, using MI-Lead can help enhance your team's own inherent motivation to complete the project. As for potential ethical considerations, would using MI-Lead in this case cause harm? We do not believe using MI-Lead in this scenario would be harmful, unless it turns out that the team does not feel that completing the project is in their best interests and you, as the leader, continue to use the MI-Lead strategies despite this. The ethical approach would be to engage the team, mutually decide upon a task (or multiple tasks) that the team is interested in working on, and then evoke reasons, ideas, ability, readiness, commitment, etc, around working on this task. As long as the team has choice and input around the tasks involved, and they see that moving forward on the project is in their best interest, we view the use of MI-Lead as being ethical in this situation.

How about in Scenario #2? What ethical issues, if any, do you see in this situation? This scenario seems similar to the first, although perhaps lends itself to more opportunity for the misuse of MI-Lead. What's the difference? In Scenario #2, it is very clear that you have a vested interest in those you lead to meet your deadline. Using the MI processes of evoking (especially evoking change talk around ability, commitment, activating language, and taking steps) and planning without first making sure that they also identify that working on the task is in their best interest, would be unethical. Only once we can establish that the individuals see that engaging in the task is beneficial and agree to discuss working on it, would the continued use of MI-Lead be ethical. The processes of engaging, focusing, and evoking (primarily evoking change talk around desire, reasons, and need) can help determine whether the individual feels aligned with the project and goals or not.

As is likely apparent, the potential for misalignment between your and the team's best interests is even greater in Scenario #3. It is clear that it is in your best interest for the team to complete the project on time, but does the team see it as being in their best interest or feel aligned with it? They might, as there are many reasons (such as a sense of pride, accomplishment, camaraderie, etc.) beyond external benefits that might lead them to view pursuing a goal as worthwhile. Having said that, the presence of the unilateral external reward identified in this scenario greatly increases the potential abuse of MI-Lead by the leader. In addition to taking the steps noted in the previous two scenarios to ensure that every member of the team sees increasing their efforts on the project as being in their own best interests or aligned with the goal, we also recommend that the leader in this situation be completely *transparent* about the potential bonus for the leader being contingent upon the team's work. This, along with emphasizing the team members' autonomy around increasing their efforts, would help lessen the likelihood of an unethical use of MI-Lead. Unless the leader can truly put the interests of the team above his or her own (that is, be willing to not get the bonus), it would be unethical to use MI-Lead to enhance the team's motivation on the project. It is worth stating the obvious here that the potential for significant personal gain can cloud one's judgment. Thus, as the leader, when such potential for gain is present, unless you are certain that you can be objective enough to determine whether you are putting the needs of the team above your own, then MI-Lead is contraindicated. Given how difficult this may be, especially in the context of significant financial or other external gain, we feel that the use of MI in many of these types of situations would be unethical.

It is much harder to make the case for the ethical use of MI-Lead in Scenario #4. There is clearly an organizational investment in the team's effort, but what about the interests of the team (or you, for that matter)? Again, the potential for putting your (and/or the organization's) needs above the team's is high, which would make the use of MI-Lead unethical. Only if you could truly honor the team's choices (including the decision to not work on the project or delay working on it to a more suitable time) and you and the team are truly convinced that moving forward on the project is in their best interests (and that you're not putting your or the organization's needs above the teams), should you consider using MI-Lead (particularly the evoking and planning processes) in this situation. Since the likelihood of these contingencies is quite low in this scenario, we would generally recommend against the use of MI-Lead in this scenario. If the leader believes there might be potential for the team to identify personal reasons for moving forward, <u>and</u> can accept the team declining to do so, <u>and</u> the leader has reason for believing that his or her own judgment has not been clouded by the organizational investment in the team's behavior, we could envision the cautious application of MI-Lead in this scenario. This would necessitate starting with the engaging process, and possibly spending more time in this process than usual given that discord is already present among the team (as indicated by the resentment they have expressed).

Once the relationship between the team and leader is established, the leader can move into the focusing process, where it may quickly become apparent that the team has no desire to even *talk about* moving forward on the project. If this is indeed the case, then moving into evoking or planning would be unethical. If during the focusing process the team members have expressed willingness to discuss moving forward on the project, and the other contingencies noted above are in place, then the leader can begin to assess whether the team sees that working on the project is indeed in their best interest by evoking ideas about desire, reason, and need from the team. If these ideas are not expressed by the team, additional evoking and planning are not ethically indicated, as the team has given the leader no indication that working on the project is in their best interest. Only if the team has given some indication of importance around working on the project should the leader then start to evoke talk around ability, readiness, and/or commitment around moving forward.

How about the final scenario, where we've finally laid the issue of conflict of interests to rest? After all, isn't it clear that working on the project is in the best interests of everyone affected? If so, what possible ethical issues could be involved in the application of MI-Lead? While it's true that moving forward on the project is apparently in everyone's best interest, it is not certain that MI-Lead would be useful in doing so. The ethical issues involved in this scenario, from an MI-Lead standpoint, would be beneficence and non-maleficence. First, as just noted, it is not clear that the use of MI-Lead in this situation would be beneficial. As we noted in Miller and Rollnick's definition, MI is about "strengthening a person's own motivation and commitment to change." If that motivation and commitment is already strong, then MI-Lead is not necessary. Second, there is reason to believe that MI-Lead could even cause some "harm" in this scenario. By spending time in the engaging, focusing, and/or evoking processes, the leader could potentially interfere with the team getting started. In this scenario, the only MI process that might be useful and avoid getting in the way would be planning, and even this process might not be necessary. One could envision a simple open-ended question ("What, if any, help would you like from me?") or complex reflection ("It sounds like you're ready to get started and don't need any assistance at this time.") to determine if any additional planning is wanted by the team.

Hopefully it is clear from the above scenarios that MI is not a tool for all occasions and that aspects of certain situations make the use of MI-Lead unethical. In wrapping up the discussion around the ethical use of MI-Lead, it is helpful to remember that MI is a powerful tool to facilitate behavior change that was developed to *help others*. It is NOT about manipulating people to achieve your goals. The use of MI in leadership situations can be particularly challenging from an ethical standpoint due to the power differential between leaders (such as supervisors) and those they lead (such as the supervisor's employees). In order to ensure the ethical use of MI in these situations, we suggest that you only use MI-Lead when you can honor the spirit of MI, and its use does not conflict with MI's pro-social philosophy.

Chapter 11

Summary and Wrap-up

Before we close, we would like to review the main concepts from the book, highlight a few take-home messages, and, for those interested, discuss how to learn more about MI-Lead. To review, transformational leader are those who demonstrate concern and compassion for the individuals they lead and motivate and challenge those individuals to be their best. The benefits to organizations that have transformational leaders include more engaged, creative, and productive team members. Our model for implementing transformational leadership is motivational interviewing, which is an approach that was initially developed to help reduce substance abuse but has since spread into multiple domains interested in promoting the health and/or welfare of others, including primary care, mental health, public health, and legal settings. MI has been studied extensively (for example, there are thousands of published articles examining the effectiveness of MI), and the evidence strongly supports the use of MI to help promote healthy behavior in the domains indicated above.

MI-Lead is a model for transformational leadership designed to facilitate motivation for and engagement in behavior and system change within an organization. It is an approach that is useful for helping bring alignment to the organization's, leader's, and team members' goals, especially when team members are experiencing ambivalence around engaging in behaviors that are consistent with organizational and/or leadership goals.

The foundation of MI-Lead is the MI spirit, or way of being with others, that focuses on partnership, acceptance, compassion, and evocation. MI recognizes that ambivalence is a normal part of the change process and that, when an individual is ambivalent about change, the more an outside agent tries to push the individual toward change, the more the individual pushes back, which makes change less likely to occur. The goal of MI, then, is to get the individual to engage more in talk about change (that is, *change talk*), which makes change more likely to happen, and to engage in less talk about staying the same (that is, *sustain talk*). The roadmap to change is laid out in the MI processes, which involve engaging with the individual, mutually agreeing upon a focus for change, evoking discussion around change, and finally mapping out an actual change plan. The skills used within each of these processes are asking open-ended questions, offering affirmations, reflective listening, and summarizing.

The application of MI to the leadership world can get tricky, especially when having to balance organizational, leadership's, and team members' agendas or needs. It can be tempting for the leader to use this powerful approach to impose his or her will and manipulate followers into doing whatever the leader sees fit. This is not transformational leadership, however; nor is it an ethical use of MI. The guidepost for the ethical use of MI-Lead is the spirit of MI, as well as the general ethical principles of non-maleficence and beneficence. To practice MI-Lead ethically, you, as the leader, must be aware of your team members' best interests, mutually agree upon those best interests, and actively work to promote them. This will not be possible in some leadership situations. This does not mean you cannot remain a transformational leader in these situations, but it will mean that you will need to draw upon different tools and approaches.

In addition to the above, we want to highlight a few key take-home messages. First, as noted above, *MI-Lead is not an approach for all leadership situations.* While our vision of the ideal transformational leader is the embodiment of the MI spirit and approach, we recognize that some situations call for different approaches, even if much of the spirit of MI remains in place. For instance, there will be times as a leader that you need to make decisions, even those that affect the team, without input from team members. There will be times when your team members are excited to get started on a project, have reasonable plans and resources in place, and do not need additional guidance or motivation from you. There will be times when you are uncertain about what truly is in the best interests of your team members, or you are certain that organizational and/or leader goals do not coincide with those of your team members. In these situations, while certain MI-Lead attitudes, processes, and skills may be appropriate, the overall MI approach would not be.

Next, *MI-Lead is not about being passive, laissez-faire, or simply person-centered.* MI-Lead is not about getting your team members to like you by letting them do whatever they want. Moreover, while MI-Lead is at it's heart a person-centered approach (that is, focused on understanding, being accepting of, and genuine with the individual you are interacting with), it is not only being person-centered. MI-Lead *is* about engaging with those you lead, but it is also about guiding them in a particular direction, one that promotes organizational and team member goals. To do that, MI-Lead practitioners must be very active, not only by constantly listening to and evoking from their team members, but also by continually tracking where the discussion is currently (that is, which MI process you and the team member are currently engaging in), where the discussion needs to go, and how to guide it in that direction.

Having said that, *MI-Lead is also not micro-managing.* The transformational leader trusts the team members, knowing that they bring expertise, experience, talent, desire to achieve, and other resources to the table. The MI-Lead practitioner taps into these resources rather than directing every aspect of them. A good leader knows when to get out of the way and let the team members do what they do best.

Finally, *MI-Lead is not easy to learn.* A good MI practitioner can make it look effortless. To an outside observer, one not familiar with MI, a conversation between a good MI-Lead practitioner and a team member can look simply like a pleasant and productive conversation, and nothing more. The observer might be tempted to think, *I can do that. That's easy...I have pleasant conversations with others all the time. It's especially easy when the other person is being so reasonable and agreeable.*

To that, we have several things to say. First, reflective listening is hard work. If you don't believe us, review Chapters 2 and 6 and try out some of the reflective listening strategies yourself. Next try adding some of the other fundamental skills, like asking open-ended questions and giving affirmations. Now try resisting the righting reflex while doing these other skills. To increase the difficulty, try doing this with a friend, family member, or colleague who is contemplating a change with which you have some experience and expertise. Chance are you will have some difficulty resisting the urge to offer suggestions, advice, recommendations, and/or your own past experiences and instead focusing on the core MI skills (primarily reflective listening). As if that's not hard enough, try doing all this while guiding toward a mutually determined target behavior, being mindful of the overall roadmap (that is, which MI process you are currently in and how and when to move into the next one).

Finally, to those thinking MI-Lead is easy because they only see it being done with "easy" team members, keep in mind that, to a large extent, you determine the attitude and the behavior of the person in front of you. That is, if you want an engaged, agreeable, and reasonable person, treat the individual in an engaging, reasonable, and agreeable manner. If you want a disagreeable, angry, and argumentative person, ignore his or her experience, expertise, and autonomy, act as though you know best, and tell the team member what he or she must and must not do.

Because MI is not easy to learn, as transformational leaders, many of you who would like to learn and implement this approach will choose to do more than read this book and practice the strategies outlined in it. To those of you who would like to further develop your skills in MI-Lead, we offer the following ideas, to be utilized as you see fit.

One opportunity to learn more about the foundation behind MI-Lead is to attend one or more MI workshops, especially those with experienced trainers who provide many opportunities for practice and feedback throughout the training. Please note that these trainings typically will be focused on MI in clinical practice, but they can still help you strengthen your foundational MI approach. When going to an MI training, we recommend trainers who are members of the Motivational Interviewing Network of Trainers (MINT), Inc. Although even attending an MI workshop is not sufficient to become a competent MI practitioner, participating in such training can help you learn and hone the MI approach and skills discussed in this book. The practice and feedback component of the training can help further develop and refine your approach. Even if the focus of the workshop is general or clinical application, additional opportunities to learn, practice, and get related feedback around the general MI spirit, principle, and skills can be quite useful in learning and applying some of the basic concepts In MI. Additionally, you may choose to seek out trainers with specific expertise in organizational leadership through MI-Lead workshops.

Another strategy is to practice the approaches described throughout this book in your interactions with others, when appropriate, and then pay careful attention to how they respond to you. If you're practicing the fundamental OARS skills to engage with friends, family members, and/or colleagues, how are they responding to you? Are they opening up or elaborating? Are they responding positively to you? Do you feel as though you're connecting with them? In short, are you engaged with them? If so, chances are you're on the right track with your implementation. If you're not getting much engagement, or if you're audience is shutting down, then you may be slipping back into the righting reflex and/or resorting to more closed-ended questions.

If you are moving on to the evoking process, say with a team member you are leading, is that individual providing change talk? Is the individual talking more than you? Is he or she doing most of the work toward change? If so, you're on target. If you're doing most of the talking or the work, or if you're hearing more sustain talk than change talk, then it may be that some additional learning, practice, and/or coaching could be in order.

Speaking of the latter, research in the learning of MI (Miller, Yahne, Moyers, Martinez, & Pirritano; 2004) has demonstrated the value of coaching and feedback. Indeed, as noted earlier, participating in an MI training alone is not typically sufficient in becoming proficient in the practice of MI. Getting coaching, mentoring, and feedback from experienced MI trainers is often a necessary component for achieving proficiency in the practice of MI. If you pursue this option, we recommend informing your coach/mentor that you are planning to practice MI in the area of leadership so they can give helpful feedback geared to leadership skills. Your coach will most likely want to observe your MI practice (either live or via watching or listening to recordings of MI interactions) in order to give you useful and targeted feedback.

One useful resource for learning more about MI and MI trainers is the MINT website (www.motivationalinterviewing.org). This website includes information on upcoming trainings, trainers in your area, and references to scholarly articles and important books, such as the 3rd edition of the seminal MI book written by the developers of MI (Motivational Interviewing – Helping People Change, 2013). In reviewing available trainings, you may choose to seek out trainers with specific expertise in organizational change.

Finally, if you are interested in learning more about MI and MI-Lead from the authors of this book, consider visiting MIforLeaders.com or contacting us at MILead@MIforLeaders.com. We would be happy to provide information on additional learning opportunities, such as training, consultation, and coaching for you and/or other leaders within your organization.

In closing, we would like to take this opportunity to thank you for reading our book. We hope this writing has provided you with some valuable guidance around implementing transformational leadership within your setting. We appreciate and commend your desires and efforts around becoming a transformational leader, and we hope that we have presented a compelling and practical model for doing so. We hope to work with you soon, in spirit and/or being. Happy and effective leading!

Epilogue

Where the Goose Leads

The Flight

Once upon a time a gaggle of Canada geese (Yes, Canada, not Canadian when talking about the goose) lived a humble life by a secluded pond. It sat hidden miles away from Crater Lake, Oregon. It was a great location because nobody wanted to see a lowly little pond when there was such a monumental attraction like Crater Lake.

In this gaggle, a medium sized gander named Edward swam across the pond, soaking in the warm fall sun. Not too far away swam a particularly graceful goose, Guinevere. The rest were on the shore eating grasses and leaves, staying close to the eldest of the group and leader, Richard. A cool autumn breeze fluttered his back feathers and rippled the top of the water.

Richard had been preparing everyone to start heading south for the winter. Each of them knew today was the day and they all felt the excitement as they anticipated stopping at all their favorite places along the way. In fact, Richard was already giving the traditional head wiggles and waggles, letting the group know it was time to start getting in formation.

"Are you ready, my love?" Edward asked his partner, Guinevere, who would be his wife if they were human, but geese don't get married. They become paired and stay with that goose or gander for the rest of their lives.

"I can't wait." Guinevere responded with her head held high, honking in the air, which doesn't sound romantic, but it sure is for geese.

"Formation! Formation!" Richard honked and flapped his wings and moved to the pond. "Everyone, formation!"

The gaggle formed a line, and Richard led the way as they moved across the water. Within moments they were in the air and in V formation.

"Another perfect take off," Gladys spoke from the back right side of the V, "great job Richard." The whole skein honked with admiration. Richard was a great leader and made sure everyone was taken care of.

That evening, they arrived at their first stop. They came in a little slower and more cautious as their regular stop had completely changed. Many of the trees were gone and grass seemed to extend every direction. Small holes could be seen here and there along with a few pits of sand. Canada geese were lined all around the small lake that sat in the middle.

The night passed quickly and was filled with joyful reunions and new introductions as they socialized for hours with many different gaggles of geese. Some were old friends, many became new ones.

In the brisk morning, dark shadows moved through the low-lying mist that clung to the ground and wrapped around the trees. Before Edward even saw what exactly was moving through the mist, one of the other geese assumed a tall, alert, sentry position and hissed, "humans!" And then an eerie silence spread across the pond like a cold mist, and all of the geese assumed the same tall, alarm position, listening and trying to see what moved through the shadows.

Some of the more edgy geese took flight, others signaled alarm by staying perfectly still, quiet and alert to the humans, and others huddled together and moved into the water. The humans were carrying something as they approached.

"Richard, what's our move?" Edward asked.

"Stay close. Be ready to move into the water." He responded.

Then chaos ensued. The humans held up strange string walls as they moved in on all the feathered friends. Geese cut the gaggle off in a rush for the water, and even more geese pushed into them, splitting up their group. Edward called for Guinevere as she was pushed away, but his calls were lost in the noise. A wall of string blanketed him and the geese around him.

"Edward!" Richard called out from just past the strange string wall. "We won't leave you Edward. We'll figure out how to get you out of there." Since geese never leave one another, even when one is wounded, it was perfectly logical for Richard to make such promises. But Edward was a different kind of goose, and he thought of Guinevere first.

"Richard. Get everyone and get out of here." Edward pushed his feathers against the strings, poking his head out through one of the small holes. "I'll find you at our next stop. Just get everyone out of here as fast as you can."

Richard gave a one-eyed stare, a look to say he was going to disagree, but he lowered his head instead, showing he was going to do as Edward wished. There were no other words spoken, and Richard left. With relief, Edward saw everyone fly off with Richard. The V formed, missing only one, him.

The humans kept putting geese in netted walls and running after others with their arms in the air making them fly away until all were either captured or gone.

The Re-Gaggle

The chaos quickly ended, as the humans caught the last of the remaining geese, loading the netted group into trucks and driving what seemed like a very long way. Several hours later, Edward found himself at an unfamiliar lake, released from his captors along with all the other geese who had been in his net. All had been released by the strange humans.

Many of the geese were still in their original groups, their families having refused to leave one another behind. Thus, all were captured. Edward began to examine his surroundings, getting a feel for what was going on around him. He wanted to escape and knew he needed to make a plan.

He noticed there were others that were all alone like he was. They appeared lost and confused. In order to make his long flight successfully, he knew he would need a new gaggle.

Edward began going from one lost goose to the next asking a few simple questions, "What happened to your gaggle? Would you like to join me in forming a new one?" Surprisingly, only seven out of the twenty that had no gaggle decided to join the group.

There was Bob, who was older and the first to join, but appeared to be rather ambivalent about it.

Next was Cathy who seemed to always have something to say and continued her honks and hinks even when there really shouldn't have been any more to add. Edward worried she may have been part of the reason others decided not to join them.

Then there was Ivan whose internal pain was immense. He was withdrawn and wouldn't so much as nibble at the roots and leaves around them. He appeared completely hopeless after losing his family and friends.

In the middle were Rodney and Liam. Both a little cranky, hissing when approached, and at first neither wanted to join the group, but when they saw Ivan join, they decided they needed to join as well.

After that, there was Sophia, who was just happy to have new friends.

Lastly, there was Julio, Sophia's little brother who didn't really say much of anything. He had a strange L shaped scar on the back of his head. Edward wanted so badly to ask what happened, but when he was looking at it, before he could speak, Sophia shook her head no, not to ask. So, he moved on and used his better judgment.

The group had their quirks and issues, but hey, what gaggle doesn't?

Engaged Goose with Direction

Edward brought the gaggle to a quiet place away from the rest of the geese. He looked over the seven, excited that he had assembled them. He assumed they would all want to find their families and friends as well and go fly south to locate them.

"I would like to tell you a quick back story about why I brought all of you together and why I need your help to fly south with me." Edward began, but before he could get any further to talk about his family, friends, and love, he was cut off by Rodney.

"We don't really want to hear any long stories. We all have our own sob stories." Rodney pushed forward and stood tall, flapping his wings, to move Edward out of the way. "Obviously we are all wanting to fly back so we just need to line up and get going. I can take the lead to get us in the air." He honked, but that's as far as he got before the whole group began making noise. All except Bob, he decided to preen instead of honk.

Liam began to argue intensely with Rodney about why he would be a better leader to begin their long journey. The other geese began debating the wisdom of flying the long distance south or whether it would be better to stay where they were for the whole year.

Edward ruffled his feathers, literally, as he listened. Then, without a word, he stood tall, stretching his neck high, assuming the familiar sentry position. All but Bob, who was still preening, stopped the noise and looked in Edward's direction.

"Rodney and Liam, we are lucky to have your determination and your skills in leading the flight! We will need both of you to help us set our course, and if you would, I would ask that you hold off until we get organized." Edward looked to everyone else. "What experience do any of you have flying south?"

Cathy spoke up first, "None of us have any experience. We don't fly south. We stay around here all year round."

"All of you just stay here." Edward acknowledged.

Bob stopped preening and looked at Edward with his right eye, "Yes, we're resident geese who stay year round."

"Amazing." Edward noted. "I've never heard of that before. What a truly remarkable concept."

"Thank you." Sophia chimed in. Her ruffled feathers began to flatten out.

"You are welcome. I wish I had known of such an idea before my gaggle flew away, including my beloved partner."

"They left you?" Liam asked, stepping away from Rodney, but not before he bumped him with a wing.

"I told them to leave. I worried about their safety, so I asked them to fly on and I would find a way to catch up with them."

"What's your partner's name?" Julio honked.

Edward was a little startled to hear Julio actually talk, and not only talk, but actually show interest in something.

"Her name is Guinevere, and I do miss her terribly." Bob went back to preening as Edward spoke. The rest of the group moved in closer.

"That's a terrible shame." Julio spoke, and if geese actually frowned, he surely would have frowned as well. "I lost my partner, Carla, a year ago while crossing one of the strange rock paths when one of those machines came out of nowhere and ran her over."

"That's terrible Julio, I'm sorry to hear about your loss." Edward lowered his head a little to give respect. Sophia put a wing around Julio.

"Thanks, Edward." Julio stood tall moving Sophia's wing off of him and gave a few flaps to look strong.

Seeing that Julio didn't want to focus on that topic, Edward moved on, "I invited all of you to join me, because I need help flying south to regroup with her and my gaggle. I understand it would be scary to fly away from your home if this is where you stay all year. But if I may, if you do join me in this flight, I'll take you to a place that is warmer than here and has a beautiful waterfall that pours into a nice secluded lake. However, it's your choice, and you don't have to join me."

Everyone was silent at first. Finally, Liam walked over to Edward to show his support. Rodney slapped his webbed feet on the way over, not wanting to be left behind by Liam.

Julio broke the silence. "I want to say yes and help you, but we've never flown south before and wouldn't know how." The rest of the group gave verbal honks of agreement, except Bob who was still involved with his preening. Edward began to wonder about Bob's constant preening, if he needed a cream or something, but he decided to keep it to himself.

"We can teach you," Liam remarked.

Cathy gave a left eye stare, "May I ask why you need us? Why don't you just fly by yourself?"

"Great question," Edward responded. "When all of us fly together, we can fly farther and watch out for one another to make sure we are safe."

"Oh?" Cathy questioned rotating her head now to give a right eye stare.

"Yes, when we fly together, that allows us to reduce the wind resistance. And when we fly, we fly slightly higher than those behind us to keep an eye out so we make sure we all stay safe." Edward appreciated her questions and wanted to give a chance for everyone to ask questions. "What other questions or concerns does everyone have?"

Bob stopped his preening and walked past everyone with his head held high. "What happens after we get there? Are we going to be dumped so you can join back with your other group?" Several of the geese dropped their heads to the ground.

"You're concerned that I'm just going to use all of you and throw you away once I get what I want."

"Yes." Bob added, "I'm not up for a journey just to be left in some new strange place."

"Thanks, Bob. I appreciate the question. All of you will be welcome to join us, stay together as your own gaggle, or follow any other path you wish."

"Sounds nice." And the preening started again.

"Other questions from anyone?" Everyone looked around, but no one said anything. "In that case, who would like to join?"

The geese all gave approving honks and hinks with their heads in the air. It was the same way they disagreed, showed they were angry or happy, and much more, but Edward knew this time it meant they agreed.

"Thanks everyone. If you're ok with it, we can talk about preparing the flight in the morning. That will give us time to build up our energy and get some rest."

Everyone agreed and went to work eating, except Cathy who seemed to be more interested in talking than eating. For the most part, everyone seemed happy.

The Focused Gaggle

The next morning Rodney and Liam woke before everyone else and were already in the water acting a bit avoidant of their new gaggle. Their attitudes seemed to match the dreary, rainy day. Each drop of moisture came pitter patting across the lake and tall trees.

Once everyone was awake, Edward invited them to the lake to join Rodney and Liam. For the most part they followed. Some straggled behind, but in the end they all made it.

There were three areas Edward wanted to help his new friends learn: 1) How to get into formation on the ground and transition in the air; 2) How to fly in the V formation in the sky; and 3) How to swap positions while flying.

The first, he thought would be easy. Edward quickly explained to everyone his plan; they would start by forming a line. He would be in the middle, and they would start on one end of the lake.

After explaining all of this, he announced that it was time to start. It didn't go well. Cathy was honking at Bob, and Bob continued to preen. Liam and Rodney became impatient, offered a few rude comments to everyone else, and flew up on their own.

Edward realized this wasn't going to be as easy as he had initially imagined. He took some time swimming while he thought about what to do, considering where to start. Finally he decided it would be best to sit down with Liam and Rodney and discuss how they could be important leaders in the group.

While the rest of the group relaxed and foraged for tender roots and grass, Edward waited for Liam and Rodney to return. When they did, he swam over to them. The sun had begun to part the clouds and only a few sprinkles still fell. The air was fresh and crisp.

"Liam. Rodney." Edward called out to them. "How was your flight?"

"Very nice." Liam spoke up first. "It was nice to get away from those incompetent geese! Honestly, I'm not sure if your plan will even work. Maybe we should just leave them and the three of us go."

"You're feeling like the whole situation is hopeless and we should just give up on trying to train all the others." Edward responded.

"Yes." Rodney and Liam spoke almost simultaneously.

"May I share a few thoughts on why it would be important to work with them?"

Liam would've given a slight frown if he had the ability, but they both gave head nods to proceed with the information.

"It's a long flight to where we are headed, and if we have a larger group it will help us fly further, keeping us safer and getting to our destination sooner." Edward hoped his argument helped them to see why it was important.

Rodney puffed out his feathers. "That would be fine, but let's look at reality. It's not saving us any time if we have to take forever training them!"

"You feel time is a moot point because of how long it will take to train them. Tell me a little more about your thoughts on how long you envision that might take?"

"Well, look at them." Rodney pointed with his right wing to the other half of their group. They were all kicked back on the grass enjoying the newly arrived sunshine. "And after how everything went this morning, I just don't see this taking any less time than a couple of weeks."

"So for both of you, you feel this group will take longer to train than how long it would take for just the three of us to fly on our own. However, you see the value of flying in a larger skein if we could train them quickly."

They both looked at one another and then back to Edward. "Yes, but we don't believe it's doable to have them trained quickly enough. Again, look at them." Rodney motioned their direction. This time Cathy had begun talking again and Bob had wandered away from the group to start preening.

"I'm curious," Edward began, "what your thoughts would be if I were to tell you that we could have them trained before today is over and be underway by morning, but that it would take both of you taking an active role in helping?"

"I would have a hard time believing it, but if you could make that happen, I would be in." Rodney remarked.

"How?" Liam added.

"If you give me the day, I'll show you. I need both of your expertise and patience to make it work."

"Ok, I'll agree." Liam relaxed in the water, dropping his head a little.

Edward began to explain his plan. Liam would work one on one with Cathy to explain the process of flying in a V shape and inviting her to take on the role of calling out each of those steps to the group. Rodney would work with Bob and also invite him to learn all the processes but ask him to take on a different role, that of monitoring everyone's progress from the back right position. Edward would take the remainder of the group and invite them to learn the process as well. Once the geese joined together to fly as a skein, Rodney, Liam, and Edward would continue to stay close to the geese or goose from their training group to provide support and feedback. Once Edward finished explaining his thoughts, he asked, "So, that's what I'm thinking. What do you feel I'm missing or that we could do even better?"

"Not a bad plan, but I'm still worried about time." Rodney added. "What if we give ourselves an hour to train our individual groups and then, if we need more time to practice, we'll let one another know, and, if we're all ready, we can start working as a large group?"

"Great idea." Edward smiled inside (because of course geese don't smile on the outside). "Almost turns it into a fun competition to see if we can all get it done in an hour. What else, if anything, are we needing to discuss before we go?"

Liam gave an odd look at both of them and flew off across the water towards Cathy, giving a loud err-onk as he left them behind. Rodney yelled out after him, "No you don't, I'll win this race."

Edward was relieved to see the two of them engaged and having fun, no longer seeming upset. They all had something specific to get done, and it seemed to be a realistic set of goals

Going for a Second Flight

An hour went by quickly and, before they knew it, Rodney, Liam, and Edward were sharing their progress. "How did it go?" Edward asked.

"Really well," Liam answered first, "because I was done first, and because Cathy did a great job. She's really excited about her role."

"You only barely beat me." Rodney exclaimed. "And I'll tell you what, Bob is going to do an amazing job watching over everyone. I've never met a goose that cares so much about others. Oh, and we took care of his incessant preening. There was a damaged feather bothering him that I helped him remove."

"Wow, sounds like both of you had some great success. My team is also doing well. What do you think, shall we give it another try as a group?"

The geese gave a couple of side looks at one another and then gave some affirmative nods. "Let's give it a try," Liam replied with a bit of excitement.

"Alright, if one of you would be willing to assemble the group, then we can get going."

Rodney flapped his wings and skimmed the surface of the lake over to the others. Moments later, they all swam back over. Cathy was leading the pack, honking the whole way, but, as far as Edward could tell, no one was really listening. As they drew close, Edward could hear her saying something about knowing a great trick that makes it look like she is walking on water.

"What did everyone think of their small groups?" Edward asked.

"It was fun." Cathy spoke first. "I'm ready to try it as a group."

"Yes, well worthwhile." Bob shook his feathers as if to show he was itch free.

"Great. And all of you should've been given an explanation of what our plan and objectives are and how we are going to work as a group. What questions or concerns do any of you have?" Edward scanned the group as he spoke.

"No questions." Cathy offered. Everyone else gathered around in agreement.

"All of you feel very confident that we can go ahead and give it another try."

"Yes, let's do it." Julio honked causing everyone else to join in with hinks and honks.

"Ok Cathy," Edward began, "take it away."

Cathy swam next to Edward. "Ok everyone. Let's line up. " She pointed her long sleek feathers to her sides. Everyone fell in. Liam, Rodney, and Edward all swam to their spots next to those they were coaching. The line up was simple. Starting from the left were Sophia, Edward, Julio, Cathy, Liam, Rodney, and Bob. "Ok, let's start moving forward." She paddled and started flapping, everyone following along.

The take off was a little rough, but, with Cathy quickly reminding people where they should fly and with Liam and Rodney supporting the group, it went really well.

Once they were in the air, forming the V took just a little bit of work. Julio took a little longer to form into the V, but Edward noticed and did a quick check in. "Julio, do you remember the next step?"

Julio looked at the other side of the V, "Oh, right, yes, thanks." He pulled back and fell into formation.

Edward was so excited that everything went so smoothly, he almost missed the fact they were flying in the wrong direction.

"Cathy." He called out. "We are a headed in the wrong direction. May I take the lead and we can practice changing positions?"

"Oh sure." Everyone shifted, and with a little guidance from Liam, Rodney, and Edward, they were all able to get back into position with Edward in the lead.

Arrival

The rest of the flight went well and when Edward spotted his gaggle from a distance his heart nearly leapt out of his feathered chest. At this point he was in the back of the V. They had shifted positions multiple times by the time they had arrived. As they came in for the landing Edward couldn't help himself, he had to do an extra roll as he entered the water.

"Edward!" Guinevere honked in joy as she flew at them. Her overexcitement caused her to miscalculate her landing and she flapped right into Edward. Their gleeful cries filled the air.

"I'm so glad you made it!" Richard swam out along with all the others. "And it appears you've made new friends. This is wonderful!"

"Yea, a really great group." Edward added with Guinevere beside him. "And if I may add, they have a great idea about how to live together in the future. They call it being a resident goose."

The rest of the story is history as the gaggles joined together and became residential geese, enjoying their small paradise for years to come.

References

Ahearne, M., Mathieu, J., & Rapp, A. (2005). To empower or not to empower your sales force? An empirical examination of the influence of leadership empowerment behavior on customer satisfaction and performance. *Journal of Applied Psychology, 90,* 945-955.

Amabile, T. M. (1983). Social psychology of creativity: A componential conceptualization. *Journal of Personality and Social Psychology,* 45, 997-1013.

Amabile, T. M. (1988). A model of creativity and innovation in organizations. In B. M. Staw & L. L. Cummings (Eds.), *Research in organizational behavior,* Vol. 10, 123-167. Greenwich, CT: JAI Press.

Amabile, T. M., Conti, R., Coon, H., Lazenby, J., & Herron, M. (1996). Assessing the work environment for creativity. *Academy of Management Journal,* 39, 1154-1184.

Amrhein, P.C., Miller, W.R., Yahne, C.E., Palmer, M, & Fulcher, L. (2003). Client commitment language during motivational interviewing predicts drug use outcomes. *Journal of Consulting and Clinical Psychology,* 71(5), 862-878.

Antiss, P. (2013). Motivational Interviewing Techniques: Agenda Mapping. *The Coaching Psychologist*, 9(1), 32-35.

Bass, B. (1995). Theory of Transformational Leadership Redux. *Leadership Quarterly*, 6(4), 463-478.

Bass, B.M., Avolio, B.J., Jung, D.I., & Berson, Y. (2003). Predicting unit performance by assessing transformational and transactional leadership. *Journal of Applied Psychology*, 88(2), 207-218.

Benson, J.D. (2015). Leadership Motivation. *Research Starters: Business (Online Edition)*, 7.

Burns, J. M. (1978). *Leadership*. New York: Harper & Row.

Deci, E.L., Connell, J.E., & Ryan, R.M. (1989). Self-Determination in a Work Organization. *Journal of Applied Psychology*, 74(4), 580-590.

DuBrin, A. J. Essentials of Management. Cincinnati: South-Western, 1990.

DuBrin, A. J. (2010). Leadership: Research findings, practice, and skills. Mason, OH: South-Western/Cengage.

Dunham, J., & Klafehn, K.A. (1990). Transformational leadership and the nurse executive. Journal of Nursing Administration, 20(4), 28-34.

Dvir, T. & Shamir, B. (2003). Follower developmental characteristics as predicting transformational leadership: a longitudinal field study. *The Leadership Quarterly*, 14, 327-344.

Feldstein Ewing, S.W., Yezhuvath, U., Houck, J.M., & Filbey, F.M. (2014). Brain-based origins of change language: A beginning. *Addictive Behaviors*, 39, 1904-1910.

Greenleaf, R. K. (1970). *The servant as leader.* Cambridge, Mass: Center for Applied Studies. Chicago.

Gumusluoglu, L., & Ilsev, A. (2009). Transformational leadership, creativity, and organizational innovation. *Journal of Business Research*, 62, 461-473.

Hettema, Steele, & Miller (2005). Motivational Interviewing. Annual Review of Clinical Psychology, 1, 91-111.

Howell, J.M., & Avolio, B.J. (1993). Transformational leadership, transactional leadership, locus of control, and support for innovation: Key predictors of Consolidated-Business-Unit Performance. *Journal of Applied Psychology*, 78(6), 891-902.

Jawahar, I.M., & Hemmasi, P. (2006) Perceived organizational support for women's advancement and turnover intentions: The mediating role of job and employer satisfaction. *Women in Management Review*, 21(8), 643–661.

Jung, C.J. (2001). *Modern Man in Search of a Soul*, New York: Routledge.

Lowe, K.B., Kroeck, K.G., & Sivasubramaniam, N. (1996). Effectiveness correlates of transformational and transactional leadership: A meta-analytic review of the MLQ literature. *Leadership Quarterly*, 7(3), 385-425.

Luthans, F., Youssef, C.M., & Avolio, B.J. (2007). Psychological Capital: Developing the Human Competitive Edge. *Oxford Press.*

Manz, C.C., & Sims, H.P., Jr. (1987). Leading workers to lead themselves: The external leadership of self-managing work teams. *Administrative Science Quarterly, 32*, 106-129.

Manz, C.C., & Sims, H.P., Jr. (1990). *SuperLeadership: Leading others to lead themselves.* New York: Berkeley Books.

Manz, C.C., & Sims, H.P., Jr. (1991). SuperLeadership: Beyond the myth of heroic leadership. *Organizational Dynamics, 19,* 1835.

McGregor, D. (1960). *The human side of enterprise.* New York, NY, US: McGraw-Hill.

Medley, F., and Larochelle, D.R. (1995). Transformational Leadership and Job Satisfaction. *Nursing Management,* 26(9).

Miller, W.R., Benefield, R.G., & Tonigan, J.S. (1993). Enhancing motivation for change in problem drinking: a controlled comparison of two therapist styles. *Journal of Consulting and Clinical Psychology,* 61(3), 455-461.

Miller, W.R. & Rollnick, S. (2012). *Motivational Interviewing: Helping People Change,* Guilford Press.

Miller, W. R., Yahne, C. E., Moyers, T. B., Martinez, J., and Pirritano, M. (2004). A Randomized Trial of Methods to Help Clinicians Learn Motivational Interviewing. Journal of Consulting and Clinical Psychology, 72(6), 1050-1062.

Pearce, C. L., & Sims, H. P., Jr. (2002). Vertical vs. shared leadership as predictors of the effectiveness of change management teams: An examination of aversive, directive, transactional, transformational and empowering behaviors. *Group Dynamics,* 7(2), 172-197.

Pearce, C. L., Yoo, Y., & Alavi, M. (2004). Leadership, social work and virtual teams: The relative influence of vertical vs. shared leadership in the nonprofit sector. In R. E. Riggio & S. Smith-Orr (Eds.), *Improving leadership in nonprofit organizations,* 180-203. San Francisco: Jossey Bass.

Pollak, et al. (2010). Physician communication techniques and weight loss in adults: Project CHAT. *American Journal of Preventive Medicine.* 39, 321-328.

Riaz, A., & Haider, M.H. (2010). Role of transformational and transactional leadership on job satisfaction and career satisfaction. Business and Economic Horizons, 1(1), 29-38.

Scott, R., Scott, G., Wolthoff, D., Shuman, L., and Cantillon, E. (Producer), & Landesman, P. (Director). (2015). *Concussion* [Motion Picture]. United States: Columbia Pictures

Scott, S.G. Bruce, R.A. (1994). Determinants of Innovative Behavior: A Path Model of Individual Innovation in the Workplace. *The Academy of Management Journal*, 37(3), 580-607.

Tierney, P. (1999). Work relations as a precursor to a psychological climate for change: The role of work group supervisors and peers. *Journal of Organizational Change Management*, 12, 120 - 134.

Teich, S.T., & Faddoul, F.F. (2013). Lean Management—The Journey from Toyota to Healthcare. *Rambam Maimonides Medical Journal*, 4(2).

W. G. Ouchi (1981). Theory Z: How American business can meet the Japanese challenge, *Addision-Wesley*, Reading, MA

Yun, S., Cox, J., & Sims, H. P., Jr. (2006). The forgotten follower: A contingency model of leadership and follower self-leadership. *Journal of Managerial Psychology, 21,* 374-388.

Meet the Authors:

JASON WILCOX is a Licensed Clinical Social Worker who loves to write and has been writing for the last eighteen years. Over the last five to ten years he has run multiple small businesses, done leadership consultation from front line supervisors to executive leaders, and is both a trainer and consultant in Motivational Interviewing. He received his Masters in Social Work from Walla Walla University. He lives in the great state of Oregon where he loves spending his time with his three cute kids, wife, and dogs.

BRIAN C. KERSH is a licensed clinical psychologist and member of the Motivational Interviewing Network of Trainers, Inc. He has been training professional staff in Motivational Interviewing since 2003 and has been involved in the development, implementation, and evaluation of numerous motivational interviewing, coaching, and communication training programs for professional staff and leaders over the years. Brian received his PhD in clinical psychology from the University of Alabama (Roll Tide!). He currently lives in New Mexico with his wonderful wife, daughter, and son.

Dr. Elizabeth Jenkins is a licensed clinical psychologist at the Tampa VA Hospital and a Courtesy Assistant Professor at the University of South Florida (USF). An active member of the Motivational Interviewing Network of Trainers and owner of Professional Health Consulting (PHC), she provides nationwide trainings in MI. In addition, she is one of the treating clinicians for the NFL's Program for Substances of Abuse. For over a decade, she has facilitated continuing education workshops for physicians on interpersonal skills building and conflict resolution through USF and the University of Florida.

Most importantly, Dr. Jenkins is a proud mom, chauffeur, chef, mediator, and confidant to two beautiful teenagers.

Made in the USA
Middletown, DE
19 April 2018